D1341843

a30213 006213865b

STUART AND GEORGIAN CHURCHES

1 Shobdon, Herefordshire, 1753 Rococo Gothic at its most fantastical

From a watercolour by Irene Hawkins

STUART AND GEORGIAN CHURCHES

The Architecture of the Church of England outside London

1603-1837

by

MARCUS WHIFFEN

B. T. BATSFORD LTD.

LONDON : NEW YORK

TORONTO : SYDNEY

To Jean

First Published, Winter 1947-8

MADE AND PRINTED IN GREAT BRITAIN
BY TILLOTSONS (BOLTON) LTD.
FOR THE PUBLISHERS
B. T. BATSFORD LTD.
LONDON: 15, North Audley Street, W.1.
and Malvern Wells, Worcestershire
NEW YORK: 122, East 55th Street
TORONTO: 480-6, University Avenue
SYDNEY: 156, Castlereagh Street

Preface

An author's first duty, at any rate in the department of literature to which this book belongs, is to define his subject. Sometimes he can do this simply enough through the medium of a title. In other cases his subject defies all attempts to affix to it a label which shall be sufficiently explanatory and yet conform to the rationing system that modern taste imposes on him in this respect. To avoid any misunderstanding in the present case it may be as well to explain that this book is concerned with the churches of the Establishment erected in England, but outside the present county of London, during the period 1603-1837.

To some critics it may seem that the limitation of its scope is too arbitrary. In Stuart and Georgian times, it will be said, leadership in architectural matters belonged to the capital; what justification can there be for omitting the London churches from your survey? The first and obvious reply is that, while books on the London churches already exist, books on the provincial churches of the period do not, so that it is extremely difficult for anyone without a good deal of time to spend on the quest to find out anything about them. Then, while it is true that some knowledge of the London churches is necessary to place the provincial examples in proper perspective, it is equally true—but not very widely recognized—that the tradition of ecclesiastical building from Elizabeth to Victoria can be studied in its full continuity and variety only in the provinces. In Wren's City churches and in those built by Hawksmoor and others under the Act of Queen Anne, London has, admittedly, two series which the provinces cannot parallel. But between the accession of George II and the Battle of Waterloo new churches in London were few and far between, and with one or two exceptions (of which the younger Dance's All Hallows, London Wall is the most remarkable) not particularly distinguished at that. Certain phases of stylistic development, notably the "rococo Gothic" of the mid-eighteenth century and the earliest Greek Revival, are not represented at all in the churches of the capital, while the small country church, which of all types was perhaps the most successfully developed during our period, is by definition absent.

What one might call the metropolitan bias of architectural historians has been among the contributory factors obscuring the wealth of Stuart and Georgian church architecture outside London. Another has been the indifference or open antagonism of guide-book compilers. (The latter state is the more desirable; I was first sent to Shobdon (I, 89), some years back, by the statement that "the church was built in 1753, and looks like it," which was certainly not meant as a recommendation). A third factor is the attitude of writers of ecclesiastical history; Abbey and Overton, in *The Church of England in the Eighteenth Century*, managed to give the impression that not one new church was erected in the provinces during that period, and to come to our own day even Professor Norman Sykes, whose excellent *Church and State in England in the Eighteenth Century* does so much to counteract Victorian prejudices, somewhat belittles the architectural achievement of the Establishment.

The purpose of this book then, is to indicate something of the quality—and the quantity—of that achievement. Primarily it is a book of information, but it is emphatically not a text-book. It is not a text-book because it does not pretend to any sort of finality. Some day, no doubt, a definitive study of the subject will be written. But before then many questions will have to be answered, and to answer them others besides myself will have to give their attention to the subject, and in circumstances more favourable to research than those obtaining in the uneasy era of war-to-peace.

Many people have made my task easier than it might have been ; the clergy, in particular, have been invariably helpful—even if sometimes frankly mystified by my interest in churches built so recently and possessing so few points of archaeological interest. My obligations to several correspondents who have supplied me with information on specific points are acknowledged in footnotes to the text. But there are three debts of a more general nature which it gives me pleasure to record here. The first is to Mr. Harry Batsford and Mr. Charles Fry for suggesting that I should write the book. The second is to Mr. Harry Batsford again, for help at every stage and in particular for the benefit of his experience and resourcefulness in collecting illustration material. The third is to my friend Mr. John Harthan, of the University Library, Cambridge, for reading parts of the manuscript and making suggestions which I was glad to incorporate in it, and for reading the proofs.

GREAT BOOKHAM, SURREY, MARCUS WHIFFEN.

SPRING, 1947.

ACKNOWLEDGMENT

THE publishers wish to express their thanks to the following individuals and authorities for their courtesy in permitting drawings and prints to be reproduced. The Banbury Guardian for Fig. 61; the Birmingham Reference Library for Fig. 48; Mr. Paul Foley for Fig. 49; the Maidstone Museum for Fig. 52; the Rev. Wm. Oliver for the figure on page 63; the Soane Museum for Fig. 104; the University Library, Cambridge for Fig. 30. The frontispiece is from a watercolour specially drawn by Miss Irene Hawkins.

The following photographers have kindly supplied photographic illustrations. Mr. F. L. Attenborough, for Fig. 88; Mr. E. J. Bedford, Lewes, for Fig. 5; the late Brian C. Clayton, for Figs. 8, 17, 26, 147; Country Life Ltd., for Figs. 138, 141, 142; Mr. Fred H. Crossley, F.S.A., for Figs. 130 and 131; Mr. R. N. Crowe, Reading, for Fig. 107; Mr. T. L. Dale, Oxford, for Fig. 78; Mr. Herbert Felton, F.R.P.S., for Figs. 10, 15, 31, 38, 132; Mr. Forrest Wompra, Middlesbrough, for Fig. 68; Messrs. F. Frith & Co. Ltd., Reigate, for Fig. 69; Messrs. W. T. Grenfell & Co. Ltd., Bath, for Fig. 84; Hastings House Publishers Inc., New York, for Fig. 58 (photograph by Mr. Samuel Chamberlain); Historic American Buildings Survey, for Fig. 42; Mr. S. A. Jeavons, for Figs. 11, 12, 90, 119, 124, 126, 146; Mr. A. F. Kersting, F.R.P.S., for Fig. 140; the Rev. J. N. Knottisford-Fortescue, for Fig. 125; Mr. C. Latham, for Fig. 6; the National Buildings Record, for Figs. 23, 24, 34, 35, 59, 62, 63, 67, 76, 80, 86, 97, 98, 99, 106, 110, 115, 116; Mr. James Nelson, F.R.P.S., for Figs. 18, 36, 37, 40, 45, 47, 64, 65, 81, 82, 85, 101, 112, 113, 117, 127, 133, 134; Mr. Sydney Pitcher, F.R.P.S., for Fig. 71; Mr. Raymond Richards, F.S.A., for Figs. 57 and 136; Messrs. Roberts, High Wycombe, for Fig. 70; the Rev. T. Romans, for Fig. 7; the late T. E. Routh, for Fig. 9; the Royal Commission on Historical Monuments (by permission of the Controller of His Majesty's Stationery Office), for Figs. 14 and 22; Messrs. J. Salmon Ltd., Sevenoaks, for Fig. 4; Mr. Walter Scott, for Fig. 108; Mr. H. J. Smith, Northampton, for Fig. 139; Messrs. E. A. Sweetman & Son, Tunbridge Wells, for Figs. 41 & 44; the late Will F. Taylor, for Figs. 16 and 27; Messrs. Vivian of Hereford, for Fig. 89; the Walpole Society for Figs. 151 and 152; Messrs. Whitney of Huntingdon, for Fig. 3; Mr. Reece Winstone, A.R.P.S., for Figs. 53, 54, 55; Mr. W. W. Winter of Derby, for Fig. 32; the author for Figs. 2, 13, 20, 21, 28, 29, 33, 39, 43, 50, 51, 66, 72, 73, 83, 91–96, 100, 102, 105, 111, 114, 118, 120, 121, 135, 143, 144, 150, 153. The remainder of the illustrations are taken from the publishers' collection.

Contents

Chapter I

Part 1 INTRODUCTORY

RATHER more than half-a-century ago Bernhard Berenson, the historian and critic of Italian art, published a short essay entitled " A Word for Renaissance Churches ". " Most of us " he wrote in it, " enjoy works of art indirectly, by association, by preparation, and above all, by finding in them what our education and general reading have led us to expect. How many good people of every possible shade of belief or unbelief manage to miss the point in Italian galleries, and come away scornful and disgusted because they have not found in a single picture either their own ideal of the Madonna, or the ideal they consider a Christian ought to have ! Even those, however, who would think it crude to look for nothing in a Madonna but a type of woman worthy to be the Mother of God, are nevertheless proud of advertising their contempt for the Italian churches of the Renaissance ' because they are not religious '." Times change, but history has a way of repeating itself, and no kind of history is more repetitive, more set in its pattern, than the history of taste. In the eighteen-nineties enthusiasm for the painting of the Italian Renaissance among English people who pretended to culture was *de rigueur* ; yet the churches of that era were, as Berenson complained, ignored or despised. In the nineteen-forties the descendants of the same people, by force of circumstances more insular in their culture, will admire almost anything which by stretching the word to breaking-point and beyond can be described as Georgian; yet somehow, here again, the churches are left out of the picture.

Why is this ? Partly, no doubt, it is because, as Berenson says, association plays so large a part in our enjoyment of, or willingness to enjoy, a work of art. We can see an English country house of the classical period as the setting for a certain kind of life, and a kind which across the years from a harsh present may appear almost paradisaical. But an English church of the same period conjures up no such agreeable picture. Few of us, I imagine, have ever experienced much desire to listen to an eighteenth-century sermon, even from the well-warmed and upholstered amenity of the squire's pew.

This is not to say that our Stuart and Georgian churches are deficient in human interest ; they have their ghosts, some of whom will walk again in the following pages. But it is to suggest that these churches must be appreciated, if they are to be appreciated at all, as works of architecture, as works of art, as expressions of the human urge to mould matter and set bounds to space. And here the aesthetic spectator, as Berenson called him, " he who is neither an architect, nor an antiquary, nor a churchman " and yet " may look at a church and . . . may enjoy the church with the acuteness of a physical sensation "—the aesthetic spectator, whom one might describe as the general reader in his other character, has been ill served by those who profess to guide him. " A brick box ";—the sneer has been repeated so often that a notion has gained currency that all our classical churches are very much alike. Yet how untrue it is! The merest glance through the illustrations to the pages that follow should be enough to reassure anyone on that point. The fact is that the English architects of the classical period, though sometimes prevented by lack of funds from realizing their conceptions in the manner they deserved, showed in church architecture a boldness and a readiness to experiment which resulted in a total achievement whose variety, at least, is scarcely to be matched in other spheres.

The reader may already have noticed that a fair proportion of the churches illustrated in this book are Gothic, and may feel inclined to question the description of the two-and-a-third centuries covered by it as " the classical period ". Yet apart from the earliest examples most of these churches, Gothic enough in style—in the superficials of architecture—are fundamentally—in the principles underlying their design—classical buildings. It needs no great sensibility to perceive that the Gothic churches of 1760 or even of 1830 are generally speaking related much more closely to their classical contemporaries than to their medieval prototypes.

The difference between Gothic and classical architecture may be expressed in a number of ways. But since one of the results of the law of gravity, which decrees that buildings may only be built from the ground up, is that every building must start from a plan—whether drawn on paper or not—it is logical that critical discussion of architecture should follow the same procedure. Now superficially the plan of a classical church may not differ very much from the plan of a medieval Gothic church. It may, that is to say, be composed of the same principal parts, chancel, nave, aisles, and those parts may be of the same general form. But to examine it more closely is to find that the classical plan and the medieval plan are the products of two quite different methods of approach. The medieval method has been described as " planning by aggregation", and the classical, " planning by subdivision". The medieval builder, that is to say, started with a single unit, the bay, and proceeded to add one bay to another until he arrived at a building of the required size. The classical architect, on the other hand, conceives his building as a whole from the first.

It will be noted that I have written " medieval *builder*", but " classical *architect*". In so doing I do not wish to appear to be taking sides in the fruitless controversy as to whether there was such a thing as an " architect " in the Middle Ages, any more than I intend to imply that a vast amount of classical architecture was not due to "builders". We are not concerned here with the producer, but with the product, and the fact to be emphasized is that, whereas Gothic is fundamentally structural, a builders' or even an engineers' architecture, in classical architecture the only valid criterion is the aesthetic one. This is not to say that the latter offers no scope for structural prowess. The contrivance by means of which Wren achieved his inner and outer domes and crowning lantern in St. Paul's is no doubt of considerable ingenuity. But in contemplating the cathedral as it stands we are not affected, one way or the other, by our knowledge of it. It is beside the point.

One of the words in the vocabulary of art criticism most often debased by inexact use is organic. However, to say that a Gothic church is organic is to make a statement which is susceptible of explanation. It is not so much that many of the *motifs* of Gothic architecture are reminiscent of natural forms, as that the relationship of the different parts of a great Gothic church is such as one finds in organic nature, so that it seems to be, like a tree, the result of a process of growth, and not of the laborious piling of stone upon stone. Then there is no one point of view from which such a building in its intricacy can be comprehended as a whole; it has, as it were, no outline—and in this it is like a tree again. But if a Gothic church may thus be described as organic, a classical one is something quite different. However complex, it is not intricate, and each of its parts, instead of seeming connected to its neighbours by the principle of growth, is in a direct relationship to the design as a whole. Ideally, a classical building has the lucidity and completeness of a mathematical equation.

The similarity, of course, is by no means fortuitous. Classical theorists, from the early Renaissance on, were at pains to show that the laws of proportion might be expressed in mathematical terms—" natural beauty is from Geometry," wrote Wren—and classical architects often consciously founded their practice on precepts thus evolved. But the real law-givers here were the "orders," Doric, Ionic and Corinthian, with their variants Tuscan and Composite. "The Orders of Architecture," wrote Sir William Chambers, " are the basis upon which the whole part of the art is chiefly built, and towards which the attention of the artist must ever be directed, even where no orders are introduced." Thus not only did " orders " seem to the classicist a *sine qua non* of any architecture worthy of the name—it is notorious that Batty Langley invented a set of Gothic orders—but the proportions of the classical orders, as laid down by Vitruvius, became so deeply imbedded in his artistic consciousness that he could only with the greatest difficulty escape from them. And so it comes about that as we look at an early Gothic Revival church we are aware that in the somewhat inadequate shadow of every buttress there lurks the ghost of a classical pilaster.

* * *

Since this is first and last a book about architecture, the term " church" is used in it in a broad, architectural sense. Generally speaking, no distinction is made between parish churches on the one hand and, on the other, chapels of ease (built to accommodate those for whom there was no room in the parish church) and proprietary chapels (built as speculative ventures). Private chapels only are as a rule excluded; they deserve a book to themselves, and since their history is so closely bound up with that of the great houses to which they are, often literally, attached, they demand a rather different treatment. However, since my eye has all the time been on architectural character rather than ecclesiastical status it may be found that I have once or twice failed to observe this self-denying ordinance.

Very few new parishes were formed during the period under discussion. The machinery for the formation of a new parish was complicated and cumbersome, involving as it did (at least until the Church Building Act of 1818) a special Act of Parliament. And so the vast majority of Stuart and Georgian churches—St. Philip's, Birmingham, (21, 48) is perhaps the most notable exception outside London—either are the outcome of the re-building of earlier fabrics or came into existence as proprietary chapels or chapels of ease. A proportion of the smaller country churches, and among them some of the most interesting, were rebuilt at the expense of a local landowner or of the patron of the living. Normally, however, a body of trustees, consisting of prominent parishioners, was appointed to oversee the work, and funds were raised by a special assessment on the parish, by borrowing, by public subscription, by the sale of pews in the new church, or by brief—or more often by a combination of two or more of these methods. When money was borrowed it was paid back over a period of years from the parish rates. Of the other methods the brief is the only one which may require explanation. A brief, then, was a Royal Letter Patent addressed to the churchwardens of the whole country, or of some specific area, appealing for contributions for some particular purpose ; it was read in the churches and a collection was made towards the object in view. As a specimen, the brief relating to Church Minshull, Cheshire, issued in 1704, may be quoted. It states :

> " That the parish church of Church Minshull aforesaid being an ancient timber structure, is so much decayed both in the roof and walls thereof that the parishioners cannot attend the service of Almighty God in the said church especially in windy weather without manifest danger and peril of their lives. And the said church cannot be repaired otherwise than by taking down and rebuilding the same ; the charges whereof according to the estimate taken by our Justices in their open sessions, upon the oath as of several skilful and experienced workmen and artificers, will upon a moderate computation amount to the sum of one thousand, three hundred and eighty pounds, eleven shillings and eightpence.
>
> " That the said inhabitants have already expended above the sum of £400 within three years last past, in taking down and rebuilding the steeple of the said church : by reason whereof, and of the poverty of the said parishioners they are utterly unable to prosecute their pious intentions of rebuilding their parish church without the charitable contributions of well disposed Christians for that purpose."[1]

Eighteenth-century briefs make it clear that many medieval churches were in a shocking state of disrepair. But the prospect of sudden death for the inhabitants of another parish was not so alarming as to cause the

[1] Quoted by F. H. Crossley, F.S.A., *Post-Reformation Church Building in Cheshire*, in Chester Archaeological Society's Journal, vol. XXXV.

congregations of that phlegmatic age to empty their purses, and the brief was an unsatisfactory means of raising money.[1]

* * *

A general note on the interior arrangement and the principal furniture and fittings of the churches of our period may be useful at this point. It is proper to begin with the altar.

In Edward VI's reign it had been ordered that every stone altar was to be replaced by a wooden table. Mary re-authorised the use of stone altars, but Elizabeth re-enacted and extended Edward's injunctions, and during her reign the table was moved for the celebration of Communion out into the body of the church. Under the high church régime of William Laud in Charles I's reign the Communion table was restored to the east end, set altarwise against the wall, and enclosed with rails to north, west, and south. (At Lyddington, Rutland, a less usual arrangement, which here represents a compromise between the Laudian edict and the vicar's puritan views, still survives from 1635; the Communion table stands some distance away from the east wall and is railed on all four sides). The main object of the rails was to ensure that the altar should be a fixture. But that there was also a need for them as a measure making for decency and order, becomes clear when we learn that in a church of the dignity and importance of St. Martin's-in-the-Fields people were in the habit of putting their hats and cloaks upon the altar, or even sitting on it, until rails were installed. During the Civil War and Commonwealth the altar rails were broken down in many churches—but by no means in all, as the large number of early Carolean examples that remain bear witness. After the Restoration, rails became once more the rule, and remained an essential feature of every church for the rest of the period under review.

After the altar and its rails, the tables of Commandments. It was ordained in one of the Canons of 1604 "that the Ten Commandments be set upon the east end of every church and chapel where the people may best see and read the same, and other chosen sentences written upon the walls of the said churches and chapels in places convenient". The Commandments are still to be found *in situ* in many churches, as often as not framed in a triptych with the Lord's Prayer and the Creed; originally they may have been flanked by paintings of Moses and Aaron, but these have nearly everywhere been destroyed or, as at All Saints', Northampton, relegated to an obscurer position in the church. Texts or "chosen sentences written upon the walls" are not quite so common, but may be found here and there; there are some early ones at Abbey Dore—a church which, although its main fabric dates from the twelfth century, has some claim to mention here, both on account of its restoration and re-fitting in 1634 (8, 123) and because the form of consecration used at its re-opening in that year was drawn up by Sir Christopher Wren's uncle,

[1] At Burghclere, Hampshire, for instance, thirty-eight briefs for various purposes were read between 1734 and 1746 and twenty-three of them produced absolutely nothing.

Matthew, who was then Bishop of Hereford. Readers of Addison will recollect that Sir Roger de Coverley " beautified the inside of his church with several texts of his own choosing ". (He also " railed in the communion table at his own expense ".)

The royal arms, either painted or carved, constitute another standard ornament of churches during our period. Sometimes they were set up over the Commandments; Professor Sykes (*Church and State in England*) quotes an early eighteenth-century writer who explains that this position was chosen " to satisfy all those who tread the courts of the Lord's House and are diligent in the performance of their duty agreeably to the contents of these grand rules of the Christian religion, (viz., the Ten Commandments, the Lord's Prayer, and the Creed) that they shall meet with encouragement and protection from the state ". The placing of royal arms in churches did not become compulsory until 1660, but the practice dated back to the reign of Henry VIII. Set up on top of the screen, or painted on the wooden tympanum which filled the space between the screen and the chancel arch, they had then usurped the place of the rood, and provoked bitter comment from Catholics of the old school. " Is it the Word of God," asked Dr. Harding of Dr. Jewell, "setteth up a dog and dragon in the place of the Blessed Virgin Mary, Mother of God, and St. John the Evangelist, which were wont to stand on either side of Christ crucified?" The screen itself was a feature of many new churches up to a later date than is often realized; several of Wren's London churches originally had screens, as had, among provincial churches of that time, Ingestre (12) and All Saints', Northampton (19). But screens of the first half of the eighteenth century are rare, and later Georgian examples, such as the Adam-rococo one at St. Paul's Walden, are generally not chancel screens proper, so much as devices to turn the chancel into a private pew for the lord of the manor.

Leaving the chancel, we move into the nave. Here the most prominent object, as was natural in churches that were (in Wren's words) " fitted for Auditories", was the pulpit. In many cases the pulpit has always stood to one side of the arch or other division between the chancel and nave, and the odds are that if it ever stood anywhere else it has been put there within the last hundred years. But the pulpit in a large eighteenth-century church almost invariably stood in the middle of the nave (19, 48). When it was so placed it certainly blocked the view of the altar from the west, and resulted in a subordination of the latter that may be rather shocking to modern taste. On the other hand the preacher in a central pulpit was not brought into undignified proximity with members of the congregation in the nearest gallery, and this seems to have been why the position was chosen—although the Commissioners appointed by the Church Building Act of 1818, one may note, recommended the lateral position, with a reading pew to balance the pulpit on the opposite side (like the arrangement initiated by George Herbert at Leighton Bromswold), which will be discussed in its place (3). The usual form of Georgian pulpit, it is scarcely necessary to add, was the " three-decker," with the reading desk and the desk for the clerk who said the responses attached: this made it possible to read the services without recourse to chancel or altar, which was only used for Communion, perhaps once a month or even less.[1]

Of the font little need be said. Always on the small side compared with its medieval counterpart, sometimes it was movable—as at West Wycombe, where it takes the form of a classical tripod adorned with the Christian symbols of serpents and doves, while an even more curious aberration occurs at Teigh (135).

This section may close with some remarks on galleries and pews. The object of the former was simply to provide sufficient accommodation without enlarging churches to impossible dimensions. Although thus justified on utilitarian grounds, they were difficult to reconcile with a strictly classical use of the orders and were always unpopular with architects; James Gibbs puts on record his relief at not having to cope with them in All Saints', Derby (32). Pews presented a similar problem, for they would hide the bases of any columns that rested on the floor or on plinths of the normal proportions. The obvious solution was to raise the columns on pedestals, pew high, and this is what Wren and his successors invariably did when a church was to contain pews. But it was not altogether a satisfactory solution. " It were to be wish'd", Wren wrote, " there were to be no Pews, but Benches "; and one or two eighteenth-century churches were in fact equipped with benches from the first. To Victorian High Churchmen galleries and pews—" pues," as the Cambridge Camden Society had it, in a spelling nicely indicative of scorn—were both anathemas, as they still are to their spiritual descendants today. But galleries often, and pews nearly always, were integral parts of a Stuart or Georgian church interior. To remove them is in most cases to make nonsense of the whole design.

* * *

In the pages that follow we shall meet with certain architects who inevitably find mention in more general studies. But side by side with these famous names we shall encounter others which, although they may crop up here and there, singly or in twos and threes, in the old topographies and county histories, or in the *Proceedings* and *Transactions* of this or that archaeological society, have not often been gathered into one company between the covers of a book. Atkinson of York, Bland of Truro, Carline of Shrewsbury, Foster of Liverpool, Harrison of Chester, Hiorn of Warwick, Keck of Worcester, Paty of Bristol, Platt of Rotherham, Pritchard of Shrewsbury, Smith of Warwick, Stephenson of Newcastle, Strachan of Bristol, Townesend of Oxford, White of Worcester, Wing of Leicester—these few, indissolubly connected as they are with the names of the centres from which their owners worked, give some indication of the nature of that company, and suggest the richness of the architectural tradition in the English provinces. Nor must we forget the amateurs— Mr. Miller, Mr. Prowse, Sir Thomas Robinson, the amiable Mr. Fortrey—who were responsible in different degrees for the

[1] John Wesley in his *Journals* describes a portable pulpit which was moved to another position every quarter so that all members of the congregation might have a chance of sitting near it.

buildings which went up in their names or at their expense ; to belittle the rôle of the amateur in the eighteenth century is to betray a fundamental misunderstanding of the ideals and methods of that age. By European standards some of these men were, no doubt, minor artists indeed. But such a building as All Saints', Newcastle, (60) for instance, is assuredly not a minor work of art judged by anything less exacting ; and, at any rate, to shut one's eyes to the pleasures of all but the highest is needlessly to impoverish life. It is one of the particular advantages of the study of architecture that even the humblest building has something to offer to him who has eyes and a sense of history. And as a class our churches of the seventeenth, eighteenth and early nineteenth centuries are almost as precious a part of the English heritage as the country houses for which those times are so justly famed.

Mappleton, Derbyshire

2 The tower

3 The pulpit and reading pew and other original woodwork

Leighton Bromswold, Huntingdonshire, rebuilt 1626-34 when the poet George Herbert held the prebend

4 The exterior from the south-west

5 The interior looking east

Groombridge, Kent, built in 1623 in thanksgiving for the failure of the Spanish Match

Chapter I

Part 2 EARLY STUART AND COMMONWEALTH

THE churches of the first period into which it is convenient to divide this book are not numerous. Nor, for the most part, are they conspicuous for strictly architectural qualities. They are the products of a time of transition—which is tantamount to saying that in looking at them one is as much aware of what they are not as of what they are. And what they are not, except in one solitary instance, is classical. Inigo Jones's "barn" of St. Paul's, Covent Garden, was the only purely classical church to be built in England during the first half of the seventeenth century. It was quite unlike anything that had been built in this country before, and in the eyes of those who saw it go up in 1631-8 it must have seemed a portentous novelty. But it had no immediate influence.

It is possible to exaggerate the significance of the Church of England's tardiness in adopting classical architecture. The desire of the High Church party to symbolize the continuity of ecclesiastical tradition may have resulted in the conscious choice of medieval forms in one or two instances. But in out of the way places Gothic was still, after all, the natural way of building, and it is in out of the way places, by the standards of those days, that many of these early Stuart churches are to be found. Had there been any necessity for a considerable number of new churches in London, things might have been different. But when a country gentleman built or rebuilt a church it was still as an act of piety and not (as it was to become later) as an exercise of taste. Indeed, if we approach these buildings from the standpoint of the man of taste we shall be disappointed. They must be seen in their historical context, as a genuine if minor expression of the spirit of their age—of the age, that is, of metaphysical poetry, of the theology of Hooker, Andrewes and their school, and of the sermons of John Donne.

* * *

Two main stylistic currents run through the ecclesiastical art of the earlier seventeenth century in England. The one, as already noted, is Gothic. The other is that brand of classicism which may be distinguished as Flemish mannerism. This peculiar style is at bottom the result of a translation of the three-dimensional conceptions of the Italian renaissance into the more linear form-language natural to Northern Europe;

fantastic and extravagant, it is characterized by a profusion of "strap-work", obelisks, low-relief ornament, and classical *motifs* used in a purely decorative, unstructural way (6).

In any particular building these two currents may exist side by side or may converge. In the case of churches, to make a broad generalization, fabrics are Gothic and mannerism informs the design of internal woodwork and fittings. The two buildings in which Gothic and mannerist elements are most completely fused fall outside the scope of this book, but compel mention because they are so often adduced as evidence by the school of thought which likes to see William Laud as the first Gothic Revivalist. Peterhouse Chapel, Cambridge, built by Matthew Wren in 1630, and the church of St. Catherine Cree, London, consecrated by Laud himself in 1630-1, are the buildings in question. Whether one chooses to describe them as "Laudian Gothic" or "Laudian Baroque" is a matter of personal preference; the terms are about equally inexact.

In the south and east of England the characteristic building material of the period was brick, and Fulmer (Buckinghamshire), Buntingford (Hertfordshire), Groombridge (Kent), and Great Stanmore (Middlesex) have brick churches of interest, though of this random selection the first and earliest—it dates from 1610—has been much restored, and the last is in a state of ruin. St. Peter's, Buntingford, is a small cruciform building, with moulded brick mullions to its windows; a tablet on the north wall bears the date 1615. The church at Groombridge (4, 5) is a simple oblong on plan, without aisles, tower or structural chancel, with a porch projecting to the south, and doorway and window tracery of stone. It too bears an inscribed tablet; this is surmounted by Prince of Wales feathers and motto and records that William, Lord Camfield, built the church in 1623 "*ob foelicissimum Caroli principis ex Hispaniis reditum*" (on account of Prince Charles's most happy return from Spain). It will be remembered that James I, under the influence of his favourite, Buckingham, conceived the idea of marrying his son, the future Charles I, to the Spanish Infanta. Had he been successful in his match-making England might have been saddled with a dynasty of Catholic Kings, so that this modest building, so thoroughly Anglican, is a fitting monument to his failure.

Great Stanmore church is both larger and later than the other three on the list. It was built at the expense of Sir John Wolstenholme and consecrated by Laud in 1632. Its font was carved by Nicholas Stone, as was also, seven years later, its founder's effigy; both of these are now in the Victorian church that has replaced it for practical purposes. As Mr. M. S. Briggs has said, Great Stanmore church is "an interesting hybrid, the battlemented tower with its turret staircase . . . . being Gothic in form, while the rest of the structure and all the doors and windows are decidedly Roman". The tower, it might be added, is often the most conservative part of a Stuart or Georgian church. And while on the subject of towers, it should perhaps also be added that those built on to existing medieval churches will not as a rule find mention in the following pages. However, an exception may be made of that of Cottenham, near Cambridge. Here the steeple fell in 1617, and was rebuilt in brick with a crow-stepped parapet and crocketed stone pinnacles of a peculiar thickened ogee form, each surmounted by a ball and obelisk, the whole affair being of considerable height and forming an unusual and striking object in the flat landscape; Dutch-looking, one would call it, but in fact there is nothing quite like it in the Low Countries.[1]

* * *

Most of the churches of this period, whatever the material of which they are built, are small. Many of them were originally chapels of ease put up by landowners for the convenience of their families and tenantry. To this class belong the "sweet little chapel", as Horace Walpole called it, at Steane, Northamptonshire, built of limestone by Sir Thomas Crewe, Speaker of the House of Commons, in 1620, and the contemporaneous sandstone church (since refaced with brick) at Lower Whitley, Cheshire, remarkable for its hammer-beam roof with scroll brackets under the beams, which was built at the expense of Thomas Tuschet or Touchet. But there are three stone-built churches, conceived on altogether more ambitious lines, which are not to be omitted from a survey such as this.

The largest is St. Mary's, Leighton Bromswold (2, 3). In its associations, this is a building of extraordinary interest, for its history is linked with one of the most fascinating episodes in Carolean Anglicanism and also touches the life of one of the three or four greatest English poets of that age.

For a detailed account of the community established by Nicholas Ferrar at Little Gidding, the reader must be referred elsewhere.[2] Even of the parish church there is little excuse to write here, because although the seating in the chancel, the brass tablets inscribed with Lord's Prayer, Creed, and Commandments, the font and a few smaller fittings survive from Ferrar's day, the fabric was wrecked by the Puritan soldiery in 1646 and now dates largely from a reconstruction of 1714. But Leighton Bromswold church, lying some four miles away as the crow flies—a good deal further by road—has been little altered.

George Herbert is generally given the credit for the rebuilding of Leighton Bromswold (2, 3). He indeed held the prebend at the time, but John Ferrar's *Life* of his brother Nicholas makes it clear that the latter played an important part in the undertaking. Herbert had tried to persuade Ferrar, since he lived so near, to accept the prebend of Leighton from him. But Ferrar was unwilling to do so, and instead (to quote the *Life*) "found the way to divert to a much righter end his Brother Herbert's good Intentions, by a Proposition he made to him—wch was, that seeing the fair Church of Layton was fallen down a long time, & lay in the dust, the vicar and Parish fain to use my Lord Duke's great Hall for y^r^ Prayers & preaching; & tho' there had been gotten a Brief for the repairing of it, the Cost estimated to be at the least upon

[1] The tower of Staines church bears the legend: "This Tower was built by Inigo Jones 1631 . . . . This stone erected 1791." It is to be feared that at the latter date the churchwardens' love of truth did not equal their local patriotism.

[2] To *Nicholas Ferrar of Little Gidding*, by A. L. Maycock, 1938.

two thousand pounds, & collections yet made, the money being not above [blank in original] pounds, could no way help the matter ".[1] In the event, Herbert " set upon it, to sollicite his Friends, & spared not his own Purse : So God in the end blessed both y^r^ Endeavours, that a handsome and uniforme (& as the Country termed it) a fine neat Church was erected, Inside and outside finished, not only to y^r^ Parishioners own much comfort & joy, but to the admiration of all men . . ." The work was supervised by John Ferrar. In July 1632 we find him writing to his brother: " We have 18 Masons and Labrores at worke at Layton Church and we shall have this weeke 10 Carpenters God prosper the worke and send mony in Amen." The prayer was answered, for the nave was completed the same year and the tower (2) to which the funds would not run, was built later by the Duke of Lennox " at his own proper cost & charges, to the Memorial of his Honor ". The chancel is that of the thirteenth-century church, whose outline plan was followed and much of whose materials were re-used in the rebuilding.

So far as churches are concerned we have not yet reached the age of the architect, and the design of Leighton Bromswold nave and tower was evidently arrived at by the Ferrars and Lennoxes and Herbert in consultation with the craftsmen concerned. " I have heer in sent a Ruff draught what I Conceive you maye Correct it where it is a miss ", wrote John Ferrar to Nicholas in the letter already quoted ; it would appear that he was referring to carpenter's or joiner's work. Externally the church as rebuilt is a brave building but rather a bare one, some fine leaden rainwater-heads constituting its sole ornament ; the tower is really handsome in its blunt and rustic way. The interior, as so often, has suffered from the stripping of the plaster off the walls, which one must picture as decorated with texts. But it retains all its original woodwork, including the reading pew and pulpit (3), both canopied and of the same height and pattern in accordance with Herbert's view that " they should neither have a precedency or priority of the other ; but that prayer and preaching, being equally useful, might agree like brethren, and have an equal honour and estimation ".

Isaac Walton, from whose life of George Herbert the last quotation comes, called Leighton Bromswold church "a costly mosaic". But this hyperbolic metaphor would be better applied to the next church to be discussed. For the woodwork and furniture of St. John's, Leeds (6), shows all that Carolean fancifulness and love of elaboration which is missing from the robust and simple carpentry of the Huntingdonshire church.

St. John's, Leeds is almost exactly coeval with Leighton Bromswold, for it dates from 1632-3. The old Leeds antiquary Ralph Thoresby tells us that it was " founded, finished, and liberally endow'd by one Person, John *Harrison*, Esq.; a Native and chief Glory of this populous Town, whose Inhabitants were grown so numerous, that the old Church, though very great, could not contain them." Harrison's endowment amounted to the then very considerable sum of eighty pounds a year, with ten

[1] This and the following quotations are from *The Ferrar Papers*, edited by B. Blackstone (Cambridge, 1938).

6 St. John, Leeds, 1632-3

7 Screen and stalls, 1635
Bishop Cosin's work at Sedgefield, County Durham

8 Abbey Dore, Herefordshire, quire screen from north-west, 1634
attributed to John Abel

pounds a year for repairs. The church he built is oblong on plan, divided longitudinally by an arcade and roofed with twin roofs. (Mr. Goodhart-Rendel has warned us against describing churches of this type as having a double nave). Outside, it is an inconspicuous enough sort of building, late Perpendicular, with nothing particularly distinctive about it. But inside, even if owing to modern restorations not everything is quite what it appears to be, St. John's is unique (6). Elsewhere—at Sedgefield, for example (7)—there may be Carolean woodwork of higher quality, but no other church of the period contains such an overwhelming display.

At Staunton Harold, where the third of our important stone-built churches stands, the case is rather different. Here it is not the joinery, excellent though that is, or even the painted ceiling to the nave, but the fabric itself that demands most attention.

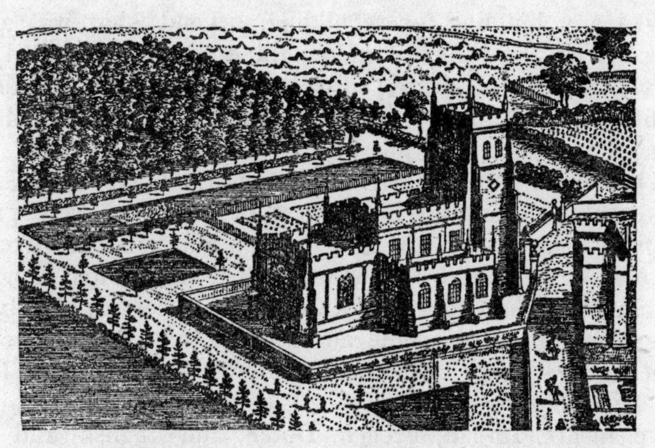

Staunton Harold, Leicestershire, 1653-63, after J. Kip

For Staunton Harold, although it was not begun until after the turn of the seventeenth century, in the middle of the Commonwealth, is a Gothic church erected by masons for whom the Perpendicular style was manifestly not a half forgotten tradition but a living and sufficient way of building. It comprises a chancel, an aisled nave of three bays, and a tower, all battlemented and buttressed in the most convinced and convincing fashion. Only the " frontispiece " containing the west doorway is classical (9). This feature, with its florid achievement of arms, life size angels and heavy swags of fruit, recalls the tomb sculpture of the time; the nearest parallels are to be found in the monuments of such men as the Marshalls, father and son, and William Byrd of Oxford. Above the doorway a marble tablet bears an inscription:

> "In the year 1653, when all things sacred were throughout the nation either demollisht or profaned, Sir Robert Shirley baronet founded this church, whose singular praise it is to have done the best things in the worst times, and hoped them in the most calamitous."

And with the cadences of that strangely poignant epitaph ringing in our ears we may move on out of the Age of Piety into the Age of Taste.

Chapter II

LATE STUART (1660-1714)

As we have seen, among the factors working against the adoption of classical architecture for church design before the Restoration was simple lack of opportunity. England was already well stocked with medieval churches, and the unsettled religious and political climate of the times discouraged any building, or rebuilding, beyond what was absolutely necessary. With the Fire of London, the opportunity arrived. Of the eighty-six churches then destroyed or badly damaged, it was decided to rebuild fifty-one. And, as luck would have it, Sir Christopher Wren was at hand to take on the job.

Wren had exactly the qualities which the situation demanded. Above all, his resourcefulness and his powers of invention were practically inexhaustible ; time and again they enabled him to make virtues of the stern necessities presented by awkward sites and limited finances. In the City churches Wren contrived a wonderful variety of plan types, free from the least trace of medievalism. And his example established classicism as the norm for English church architecture. To define Wren's " style " in the narrow sense is not easy, for it contains many different elements, Italian, French, Dutch, and English, and does not lend itself to pigeon-holing under any of the ordinary labels. If we fall back on a term much used—and misused—today, and call it baroque, someone is sure to point to some building which might almost have been designed purposely to refute our classification—such as St. Stephen Walbrook, undoubtedly one of Wren's masterpieces yet serene enough to delight the Palladian Lord Burlington and the Greek Revival sculptor Canova. And, indeed, only in certain of his later works does Wren show himself a baroque master. His style in general is best called, simply, Wren.

* * *

Several churches outside London have at one time or another been attributed to Wren. But the claims of two only will bear scrutiny. Of these, St. Mary's, Ingestre, is the earliest, while it also shows the greatest number of Wren characteristics (11, 12, 126, 144).

A faculty to rebuild the ruinous church of Ingestre was granted to Walter Chetwynd, the lord of the manor, in 1673. Work began the same year ; the new church was finished in 1676, and consecrated by the Bishop of Coventry and Lichfield in August 1677, after which ceremony Chetwynd gave a " splendid dinner at the house for the Nobilitie, Clergy

9 Staunton Harold, Leicestershire, 1653-63 A "frontispiece" in the style of the tomb sculpture of the time

10 Willen, Buckinghamshire, 1679-80, by Robert Hooke The base of the tower, with doorway deriving from French classical models

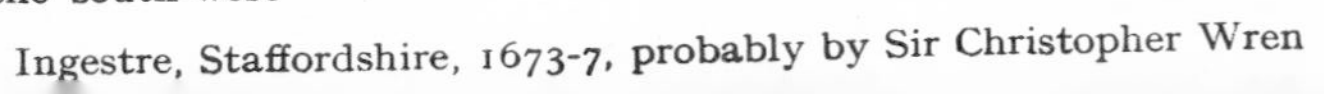

11 The exterior from the south-west

12 The interior looking east

Ingestre, Staffordshire, 1673-7, probably by Sir Christopher Wren

and Gentry, both men and women, of the whole country in a manner, which came in that day to see the solemnity performed". The quotation is from Plot's *Natural History of Staffordshire,* and it is Dr. Robert Plot, indeed, who forms the chief link between Wren and the remote Staffordshire parish of Ingestre. For he was secretary of the Royal Society when Wren was president, and he was encouraged to produce his work on Staffordshire by Walter Chetwynd.

The editors of the Wren Society's nineteenth volume go so far as to suggest that Plot's account of Ingestre church may have been supplied by Wren himself. Whether that was so or not, it has the interest of all contemporary descriptions of buildings that were the latest thing in their day, and a lengthy extract may be excused. Ingestre church was built, we read, " in the form of a *parish-Church* not great, but uniform and elegant . . . The *Chancell* within paved throughout with black and white marble, the *Windows* illustrated with *Armes* and matches of the *Chetwynds* in *painted glass* : and the *Ceilings* (144) with the same in *Fretwork* . . . . The *Navis* or body of the *Church* separated from the *Chancell* with an elegant *skreen* of *Flanders Oak* (126), garnisht with the *Kings Armes* ; and great variety of other curious *carvings* at the *South* corner whereof stands the *Pulpit* (128), made of the same wood, adorned in like manner with *carved* work, and the Ironwork about it curiously *painted* and *guilt.* The *Seats* are also made of the same *Oak,* all of equal height and goodness throughout the whole *Church,* the lord himself not sitting in a finer *Seat* (only somewhat larger) than the meanest of his *Tenants* ; so humble is this truly Wise man, in the midst of all this *magnificence.* Near the entrance on the left hand, stands a curious Font all white marble, the whole *Church* too being cieled with the finest plaister, garnisht also with deep and noble *Fretwork* . . . ."

Little has been changed, and not too much added, since 1677. Ingestre church is almost as ornate as the richest of Wren's London churches, and incomparably the most elaborate country church of its time. Built of stone throughout, it consists of nave and aisles of four bays, a western tower, and a spacious chancel ; the only entrance lies through an elliptical vestibule in the tower. As Plot (or Wren) says, it is "not great", but it has a presence beyond its actual dimensions. Especially is this true of the interior, where the clustered columns supporting the arcades are a particularly successful feature. Granted the necessity of raising their bases above the pews, correctly proportioned columns set singly would have been inadequate here. By quadrupling them, the architect has achieved a dignified effect on a very small scale. The treatment of the arcades as a whole, with the circular clerestory windows above, is reminiscent of St. Bride's, Fleet Street, in which, however, the columns were only paired and the central space was covered by a barrel vault instead of a coved ceiling. The character of the carving, whether in stone, wood or plaster, is better conveyed by the photographs than by any description ; it has all the vigour and fullness of relief of the best work of the period.

The other country church which is attributed to Wren with a fair measure of probability is a much simpler building, of brick with stone dressings. It stands at Farley, Wiltshire, and was built at the expense of Sir Stephen Fox *circa* 1690. Unfortunately no documents survive to provide us with certain evidence as to its designer. But Fox, who was Paymaster-General from 1661-79, was at the time a Commissioner of the Treasury and as such connected with Wren in the building of Chelsea Hospital. What is more, the extant building accounts relating to the almshouses and warden's house at Farley, also erected by Fox in the sixteen-eighties, show that the direction of that work was put into the hands of Alexander Fort, who was Wren's master joiner, while the names of other of Wren's workmen also appear in the pay-rolls. Thus the obvious supposition is that Farley church also was built by Fort, and to Wren's design.

If we grant, as we may, that Wren was the "architect" of Farley church, we must remember that perhaps all he did was to rough out its main lines. In a building of minor importance the details could safely be left to the workmen on the spot, guided by Fort or whomsoever the general director of the building operations might be. By this time there were plenty of masons who were perfectly capable of carving a capital or profiling a cornice without the help of detailed drawings by the architect who "drew the model" of the building on which they were engaged. Sometimes their work was crude enough; not all the detail of Wren's City Churches will stand up to critical examination. But their competence and initiative made possible the speedy diffusion of classical architecture.

However, we know that Robert Hooke, in designing Willen church (15), which was built in 1679-80 at the expense of Dr. Busby, the celebrated master of Westminster School, left very little to chance, or to the whims of his workmen. For his diaries contain many references to this church. On November 22, 1678, Hooke was "all day about Dr. Busby's module of a church"; on December 11 in that year he gave Busby "another design for a church"; on March 25, 1679, he "dined with Dr. Busby, Dr. Fell, etc., agreed about country church" and in April he "drew mouldings for Dr. Busby". These references, and a number of others like them, make it clear that Hooke was concerned to make this little building as good as he knew how.

Hooke's name is familiar to many because of his scientific attainments. His architecture is less well known, for the simple reason that a great deal of it, including Bedlam Hospital, Montagu House, and the theatre of the College of Physicians, has been destroyed. He was a personal friend of Wren, and also his assistant, in a capacity which at this date it is impossible to define exactly, in the rebuilding of the City churches. But he was no great architect. His work is that of a clever man who knew the rules but was without much real creative power; it is what Wren's might have been had not Wren had genius. Willen church has obvious faults. The nave and the tower are ill related and the latter is a rather top-heavy and graceless composition (15). (Originally it was surmounted by a cupola, of wood and lead or copper, which possibly helped the general effect.) The sculptural, cave-like doorway in the base of the tower (10) is of a type used by Wren, and later, with superb effect, by Hawksmoor ;[1] Wren probably took the *motif* from François Mansart's Hotel de Conti (1645), which he would have seen on his French visit. Inside the church there is much to please the eye in the way of craftsmanship—an elaborate plaster ceiling, a handsome marble font with a carved oak cover (132), and an organ-case and other joinery of the time.

There are other country churches of this period about whose authorship nothing seems to be known. Honington for example, in Warwickshire. This church was built at the expense of the Parker family, of Talton, Shipston-on-Stour. It consists of apsidal chancel, aisled nave and western tower (of which the lower part is medieval) and contains much good carved woodwork (125). Then, little known but even more remarkable, there is the church, in the park, at Euston, Suffolk, built by the Duke of Grafton in 1676 (13). Its west tower, nave and chancel of equal length and broad transept lead one to describe this as a cruciform building, for although as a matter of fact the north-west and south-west angles of the cross are filled in with aisles to the nave, these are given a certain independence of the main design by being lower than the rest of the structure and separated from it by massive piers, so that they do not detract from the cruciform effect of the whole. The body of the church is ceiled with ribbed cross-vaults of plaster and the nave lit by a clerestory of circular windows. Here too there is woodcarving of more than ordinary merit, in addition to ornamental plasterwork which includes an exceptionally pretty floral ceiling in that part of the south aisle which contains the founder's tomb (143).

* * *

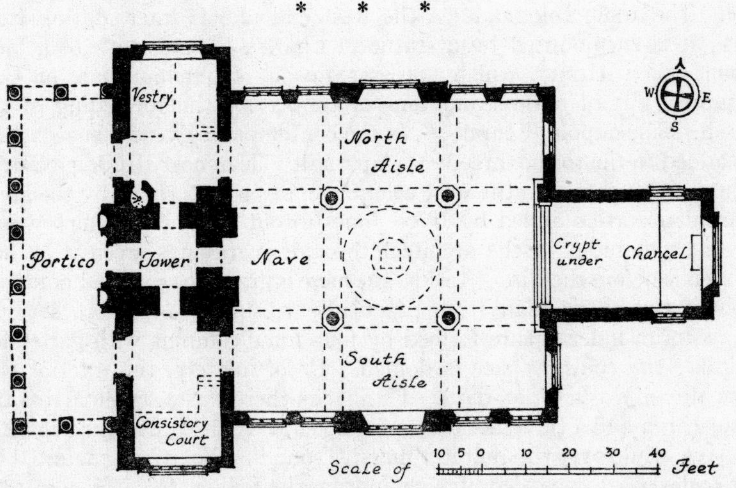

All Saints' Church, Northampton, 1676, with portico added 1701
The base of the tower is medieval

The two largest provincial town churches of the late seventeenth century both owe their existence to the same cause as Wren's St. Paul's and City churches. On September 20, 1675, three quarters of the town of Northampton, including All Saints' church, was ravaged by fire ;

[1] In St. Mary Woolnoth.

nineteen years later Warwick, with St. Mary's, experienced a similar disaster. As might be expected, the name of Wren has been associated with the rebuilding of both Northampton and Warwick churches. In the case of the latter there exists tangible evidence that he was interested, although he did not, as things turned out, design the present church. But All Saints', Northampton, must be taken first.

In this case the Wren connection is tenuous indeed. No documents remain, and the suggestion that Wren may have provided the design is based on the resemblance of the plan of All Saints' to that of St. Mary-at-Hill, which was completed in 1676. This resemblance can hardly be coincidental, but it does not follow that Wren was the architect of All Saints'. It is possible that the churchwardens and other prominent parishioners visited London to see what the new churches were like, and that St. Mary-at-Hill took their fancy and was recommended as a model for imitation to the man who was given the task of rebuilding All Saints'. But if Wren is ruled out, who was responsible for the church? The name of Henry Jones has been put forward. Although there is no real evidence, Jones is a possible candidate. He was a local man, a carpenter by trade. He is mentioned in the correspondence of the Ishams of Lamport, where he is called " architectus Northamptonae " and is stated to have built Haselbeach Hall (since destroyed); he died in 1721 at the age of 72.

The new nave of All Saints', Northampton, was opened in 1680, and the mayoral chair which is the finest of its remaining fittings bears that date. The Ionic colonnade at the west end (20) is later, dating from 1701; it is surmounted by a statue of Charles II, the work of a local mason called Hunt,[1] which was set up in commemoration of that monarch's gift of a thousand tons of timber for the rebuilding of the church. The cupola ("cupiloe", as the contemporary vestry book has it) was added to the tower three years later still. The most striking external feature of the church is the west colonnade, inspired perhaps by the great Corinthian portico added by Inigo Jones to old St. Paul's, which would have been familiar to the architect through engravings, even if he had not seen it before the Fire. Inside, the nave is grand in scale and pompous in conception. On plan it is practically a square of about seventy feet, with an inner square formed by four Ionic columns with garlanded capitals; the central space is domed. Unfortunately, the interior was twice altered in Victorian days. Until 1865 there was a screen across the chancel arch and a three-decker pulpit stood in front of it in the centre of the nave, while over the pulpit a massive sounding-board, surmounted by four eagles, was suspended by a chain from the ceiling (19). Then in 1888 the chancel arch was remodelled, the coupled columns on either side were added, and—as if to draw attention to the lamentable clash in scale between those columns and the much larger order of the nave—the present pilasters were built against the nave walls. But perhaps we should be grateful that so much (including the elaborate plaster ceiling of the chancel) has come down intact. All Saints' is by no means a subtle

[1] John Hunt, sculptor also of the handsome monument, with two standing figures, to Sir William Boughton in Newbold church.

13 Euston. Suffolk, 1676

14 All Saints, Oxford, 1707-10, by Henry Aldrich, Dean of Christchurch

15 Willen, Buckinghamshire, 1679-80, by Robert Hooke

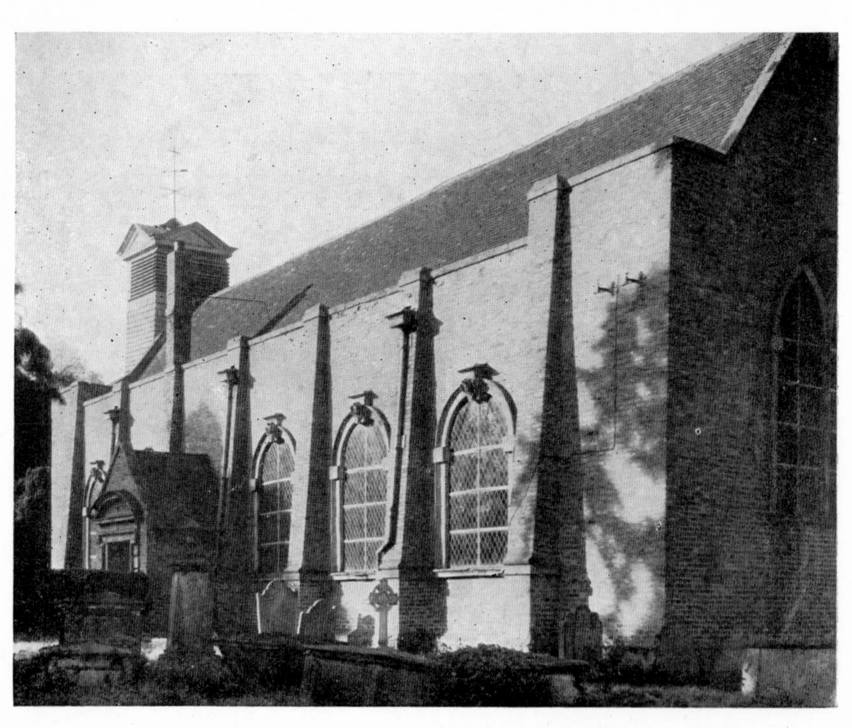

16 Minsterley, Shropshire Rural classicism of 1692

design, but it has more than its share of that robust vitality which even the minor works of its age possess.

When, in 1694, fire swept through Warwick, all but the chancel of St. Mary's church was damaged beyond repair. The town's total loss from the fire, we are told, "was computed at £90,600, towards which they gathered by a Brief £11,000 and Queen Anne gave them £1,000 more, with which they rebuilt their Church and Steeple, and very little came to the relief of the poor Sufferers"; the tower alone cost £1,600. As mentioned above, Wren was interested in the rebuilding of the church. At All Souls' there are half a dozen most interesting drawings of four different schemes—all Gothic—for a new St. Mary's, and Sir Christopher's son, in the catalogue of designs in his *Parentalia,* lists an "Orthography of the Tower of the parochial church of St. Mary at Warwick, erected after an unsuccessful Attempt in Execution of a defective Design by other Hands". There is a mystery here. Certainly the first attempt at the rebuilding of the tower of St. Mary's ended in disaster. But, equally certainly, the designer of the nave and the tower of the church as it stands today was Sir William Wilson, and the work was carried out by the Warwick builder family of Smith.

Sir William Wilson (1641-1710) was the son of a Leicester baker. Like many before and after him he was a mason-architect, and a number of monumental effigies and mural tablets from his hand are known. Few buildings can be ascribed to him at present, although research will probably reveal more. Perhaps the most notable, apart from St. Mary's, is Sir John Moor's school at Appleby, and there, as apparently in the case of St. Mary's, his design was preferred to one by Wren. Of churches, that of Weston-under-Lizard, rebuilt in 1700, may be his. Why Wilson was knighted remains obscure. The Nottingham historian, Deering, states that "a Leicestershire widow lady, the lady Pudsey, who was possessed of a very large jointure, falling deeply in love with him, got him knighted and married him, but he living up to the extent of his apron-string estate, and his lady dying before him, Sir William returned to his former occupation, and the publick recovered the loss of an eminent artist". There are at least two errors in this, for Jane Pudsey came of a Warwickshire family and Wilson did not abandon practice, either as sculptor or as architect, during her lifetime. Yet, if architecture may be accepted as evidence of character, one can well believe that Wilson "lived up to the extent of his apron-string estate". For St. Mary's has a splendid swagger which is assuredly not the expression of a niggardly soul. The historian of style is confronted by it with the question; Gothic Revival or Survival? The answer must be: Both. St. Mary's is a Gothic Revival building in that by the date of its erection Gothic was no longer the natural style for a large church, but was here consciously adopted to harmonize with the surviving medieval chancel and to put the citizens of Warwick in mind of the ancient dignity of their town; we may be sure that the balustrades and urns and classical niches came to Wilson more easily than the Gothic arches and pinnacles, while for his window tracery he apparently had resort to French models, such as St. Eustache in Paris. On the other hand the architecture of St. Mary's has a dynamic which is truly Gothic in essence, and this is surely a Survival. To appreciate the difference between Wilson's Gothic and that of an age when the rule of classicism had stifled the Gothic spirit, one should imagine the tower of St. Mary's as the later eighteenth century might have designed it, with heavy cornices breaking it into precisely defined storeys and the niches, which in Wilson's design chase each other skywards with such careless freedom (26), judiciously grouped in pairs and ranged with the arches and openings in the centre of each of the tower's four walls. In short it is possible to see St. Mary's, Warwick, which was completed in 1704, as the final flourish of English Perpendicular architecture.

* * *

Certain churches of Charles II's reign are scarcely distinguishable from those built thirty, fifty, or even a hundred years earlier. In out of the way places local masons continued to work in the tradition of their grandfathers. The buildings which they put up have not much historical significance, nor are they very considerable aesthetically. But although in more than one sense they belong to the byeways rather than the highways, they have their own interest.

The church at Compton Wynyates, for instance, is in certain respects a smaller, rural edition of St. John's, Leeds. It was built in 1663, the former church having been destroyed in the Civil War. It is planned as a rectangular nave with a western tower ; there is no chancel. The nave is divided down the middle by an arcade of four bays and covered by twin roofs with barrel vaulted ceilings inside (18). Neither the arcade nor the mullion windows, with their trefoil-headed lights and drip-mouldings, nor the stepped buttresses, set diagonally at the angles of the nave, made any concession to modernity. Classical forms appear only in the shaping of the upper courses of the nave walls into the rough semblance of an entablature, in the thin pilaster-like projections, with their strapwork ornament, dividing the walls horizontally between the windows, and in the emphatically treated voussoirs of the south doorway.

One of the latest examples of Gothic survival is provided by the church of Monnington, Herefordshire, which was rebuilt in 1679-80 at the expense of a local worthy Uvedall Tomkyns. Its plan is that of a small medieval church, with nave and chancel under separate roofs, west tower, and north porch (17). Absence of angle buttresses gives the church, which contains a coeval screen and other interesting joinery, a slightly skimped appearance, but it would be hard, on the evidence of style alone, to date it even approximately.

The nave of Newent church, Gloucestershire, on the other hand, is the outcome of an ambitious attempt on the part of local craftsmen to produce something modern. Its erection was made necessary by the collapse of the medieval structure under a great load of snow in January 1673. Charles II granted sixty tons of timber from the Forest of Dean towards the new nave ; a list of subscribers to the work, which was begun in 1675 and completed in 1679, may still be seen in the base of the tower. The builder was one Edward Taylor, a carpenter, who is said to have

17 Monnington-on-Wye, Herefordshire, 1679-80

18 Compton Wynyates, Warwickshire Built in 1663 to replace the building destroyed in the fighting of the Civil War

19 The interior before the 1865 alterations From a lithograph of *circa* 1850

20 The west portico, added in 1701

All Saints, Northampton, 1676-80

worked under Wren on St. Bride's, Fleet Street.[1] With what seems extreme audacity—when one considers the cause of the collapse of the old nave—he undertook to cover the whole space formerly taken by the nave and south aisle with a single roof having no internal supports between the outside walls. The system of trussing he adopted was invented by Wren some thirteen years before for the roof of the Sheldonian Theatre at Oxford, which at the time seemed a marvel of ingenuity. In the event, Taylor's boldness was justified, for his roof lasted until 1906, when it had to be renewed on account of decay in the outermost timbers, caused by water leaking in through defective gutters. The general appearance of the interior of his nave has suffered from the stripping off of the plaster in the nineteenth century. With its Ionic pilasters on very high pedestals and no entablature, it is a curious rather than beautiful example of vernacular classicism, although certainly magnificently spacious.

By the time of the "Glorious Revolution" of 1689, classicism of a sort was established even in relatively backward places. It was not, perhaps, a very refined sort, but what it lacked in elegance it made up for in vitality. There is a little church at Minsterley, Shropshire, which was built in 1692 and shows what the provincial mason could then accomplish without benefit of architect (in the modern sense) (16). Only in the steep gables over the east end and the south porch, and in the sloping buttresses along the sides, is there anything that might be called Gothic. The round-headed windows with their cherub-head keystones, the pedimented doorway, and the frontispiece to the west with its segmental pediment and elaborate if crude carved stonework, belong to a brand of classicism which was to live on in the provinces well into the 'thirties of the next century.

Henry Bell of King's Lynn, one of the most distinguished of our provincial architects, was born in 1653 and designed his most famous building, King's Lynn Custom House, when he was thirty. Thus he was by birth and training a man of the later seventeenth century. But several of his known works belong to the early years of the eighteenth, and among these is the church of North Runcton, four miles from Lynn. The old church here was, in the words of the brief appealing for funds for the new one, " beaten down flatt to the ground by the fall of the steeple " in 1701. Bell was one of the trustees nominated to take charge of the rebuilding, and besides providing the design, he subscribed towards the work £15—only £5 less than Trinity College, the owners of the living. His church, which was not completed until 1713, is in some respects not unlike a miniature version of All Saints', Northampton, with a square nave, a deep chancel, and a western tower (28). In the nave stand four Ionic columns and these have the garlanded capitals of a type which Bell employed elsewhere and which we have also noted at Northampton. The central space between the columns, which support lintels, is covered by a square dome formed by intersecting vaults ; the ceiling of the chancel

[1] According to the booklet provided in the church. But his name is not found in the volumes of the Wren Society.

is flat and its walls are lined with oak panelling, architecturally treated with Corinthian pilasters and entablature.

Although resemblances between the works of the two men are probably to be ascribed to common sources of inspiration as much as to anything else, Bell can in a general way be said to belong to the School of Wren. North Runcton church at any rate has an obvious affinity with the City Churches. But early in the eighteenth century a new style appears in English architecture. The later work of Wren himself was affected by it, but it is associated more especially with the names of Sir John Vanbrugh and Nicholas Hawksmoor. Its most obvious characteristic is an unprecedented bigness of scale ; to this is added a closer interdependence between the elements of design, which detached from the compositions of which they form part would after seem meaningless or grotesque. In general it is a style of bold silhouettes and sculpturally treated masses, expressing a new sense of the possibilities of drama in classical architecture and an attitude to classical forms which is not uncoloured by the associations attaching to their Roman ancestry.

In Vanbrugh's masterpieces, and in Hawksmoor's London churches, this native baroque produced some of the most moving architecture of modern Europe. Confining our view to English churches outside London, we shall not find much that is comparable to these. Characteristically enough of the eighteenth century, the first church to reflect the new manner was designed by an amateur, that " polite, though not profound scholar, and jovial, hospitable gentleman " (to quote Macaulay), the author of a treatise on logic which remained a standard text-book for a hundred and fifty years, the catch-singing, pipe-smoking Dean of Christ Church, Henry Aldrich.

All Saints', Oxford, was begun in 1707 and finished in 1710, the year of its architect's death. The nave is a substantial, four-square block with a Corinthian pilaster order and a windowed attic above the cornice. As Mr. Goodhart-Rendel has said, " the division of its walls into two storeys signifies nothing without or within except that its designer, having made those walls very high, did not know how else to deal with them ". For the interior, irreverently described by another writer[1] as "like a hat-box seen from the moth's point of view", is simply a large hall, about 70 feet long by 42 broad by 50 high, with pilasters repeating those outside but neither columns nor galleries (14). The steeple (22) invites comparison with Wren's London steeples, and it may be objected to it that the square tower and circular superstructure are too independent of each other, although the latter is pretty enough if regarded as a separate composition, an addition. To quote Mr. Goodhart-Rendel again, the design of the church as a whole " is the work of a talented amateur, and appropriately shows both talent and amateurishness ". But if we would give Aldrich his due we must recognize that All Saints' was unlike anything previously seen in England, for Wren had never wrapped a Corinthian order round a church in this way. Although the design is manifestly the product of an academic rather than an imaginative approach to architecture, and although Aldrich in his writings professed allegiance to

[1] Christopher Hobhouse, *Oxford* (Batsford), p.77.

21 St. Philip, Birmingham (now the cathedral), 1709-15 (tower completed 1725), by Thomas Archer

22 All Saints, Oxford, 1707-10, by Henry Aldrich

23 The exterior from the south-west

24 The interior, looking north-east

St George, Great Yarmouth, 1714, by John Price

Palladio, the scale and proportion of its components relate it more closely to the Vanbrugh-Hawksmoor baroque than to anything else. The interior of All Saints' might be a hall in Castle Howard or Blenheim Palace.

Thomas Archer is a more considerable architect who in recent times has been styled an amateur. Sir Lawrence Weaver, for example, thought that he "was one of the men of the early eighteenth century who seems to have adopted architecture as a fit employment for a person of taste, rather than as a serious and absorbing profession". But the fact is that the inverted snobbery which held that Burlington, being a lord, could be no architect, has told against Archer's reputation also. For Archer, if not a lord, was at least the uncle of one, and himself a person of importance at Court. As Groom-Porter, he was official supervisor of gaming throughout the kingdom, and to that office, and to his other post of Comptroller of the Customs at Newcastle, he may have owed much of the £100,000 he left at his death. But although he was not dependent on the practice of architecture for his living, Archer was surely not an amateur in the sense that Aldrich was. Far from being one of the Single-Speech Hamiltons of the art, he has quite a considerable list of buildings to his credit. His contemporaries certainly took him seriously. When in 1713 political causes led to the temporary suspension of Vanbrugh from the Comptrollership of the Works, the Duke of Shrewsbury recommended Archer as his successor. "Impartially speaking", he wrote, "he is the most able and has the best genius for building of anybody we have."

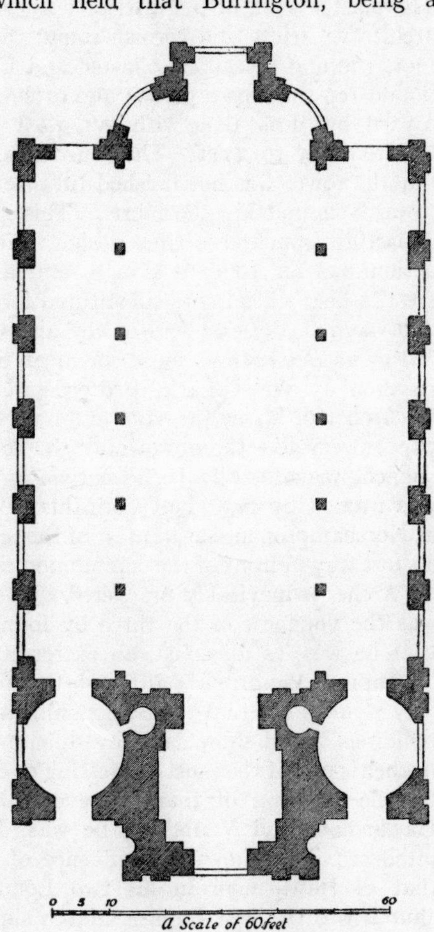

St. Philip's, Birmingham, 1709
Thomas Archer, architect
Plan from *Vitruvius Britannicus*

Archer designed three important churches. Two of them, St. John's, Westminster, and St. Paul's, Deptford, do not concern us here. St. Philip's, Birmingham, which does, is the earliest of the three.

St. Philip's, Birmingham, (now the cathedral), (21, 48) is one of the few churches that appear in Colen Campbell's *Vitruvius Britannicus*, although its baroque cannot have been sympathetic to the Palladian Campbell. It was designed in 1709. Archer, whose family seat was at Umberslade, near Tanworth-in-Arden, was appointed architect by a Board of Commissioners, consisting mainly of local gentry, of which he himself was a member. The proceedings of this board, together with the building accounts, have been preserved. A William Shakespear, of Rowington, was contractor for 200 cart-loads of stone, the Rowington quarry having been chosen in preference to "Mr. Archer's quarry". The plaster work of the interior was executed by Richard Hass (". . . . architrave, frieze and cornish round the said aisles for half-a-crown the foot, running measure; pilaster and Corinthian capitals fluted for one pound ten shillings a piece; and architrave round the arches for 1s. 6d. a yard, but if not done with hair, 1s. a yard . . . ."). Hass's agreement is dated May 16, 1711. The church was consecrated on October 4, 1715, but the tower was not finished till after 1725, when George I gave £600 towards completing the fabric. This gift was responsible for one small departure from the original design. For the intermediary in the transaction was Sir Richard Gough, and a weather vane incorporating his crest, a boar's head, was substituted for the cross at first proposed. The doorways at the east end of the aisles were also altered in execution; *Vitruvius Britannicus* shows them as duplicates of the doorway of the pavilion at Wrest Park, Bedfordshire, an ambitious garden building by Archer of about the same date as St. Philip's and with a dome and cupola very like those crowning the tower of the church. The present chancel was added by J. A. Chatwin in the 1880's. Before then the altar was framed by two giant Corinthian pilasters and the pulpit stood, as at Northampton and as in most of the larger eighteenth-century churches, a short way in front of the communion rails in the middle of the nave (48).

Archer is inevitably bracketed with Vanbrugh and Hawksmoor. He was the youngest of the three by four years. It is usual to make out that he was, as an artist, an extremely poor third—to dismiss him as "a pupil of Vanbrugh", although the most rudimentary sense of chronology would show that to be impossible and comparison of their respective buildings would show as many differences as resemblances. In reality, Archer is one of the most interesting of our architects. Although, judged by the criterion of total achievement, he must take a place below Hawksmoor and Vanbrugh, he was, I think, the latter's superior in intellect; if he shows the influence of any English contemporary, it is that of Hawksmoor in his two London churches. His Birmingham church was the first English church since St. Paul's, Covent Garden, to have been built by an architect who had had the advantage of Italian travel. And it should be remembered that it preceded Hawksmoor's first church, St. Ann's, Limehouse, by three years.

The tower of St. Philip's (21) received its due of praise from Sir Reginald Blomfield, who pointed out that it shows that Archer "deliberately rejected Wren's favourite device of getting his effect by constant repetition of storeys". It is a fine thing which at present suffers a good deal from the blurring of its detail caused by the extreme decay of the stonework. Oddly enough, its incurved sides are almost unique in this country; one would think that English architects had avoided the *motif* on principle. The stonework of the body of the church was completely renovated by Chatwin. Here also is much that will repay careful examination. The horizontal banding of the walls, contrasting with the strong verticals of the pilasters, may recall the entrance front of Castle Howard, but it is also a feature of Archer's Heythrop Hall (*c.*1705). Most interesting of all, perhaps, are the doorways to the entrance lobbies which flank the tower, with their pedimental sections of cornice resting on splayed triglyphs over polygonal jambs whose mouldings are almost Gothic in their saliency; Archer, alone of English architects, broke up and reassembled the stock forms of classical architecture in this daring manner, which suggests more than a passing acquaintance with the late baroque of Rome and Northern Italy. Inside the nave is almost austere, enrichment being confined to the capitals of the pilasters at the west end, the foliated keystones of the arches, and the boldly modelled cornice above. The arcades and tower arch impart a noble rhythm to the whole interior, but it must be confessed that Archer made little attempt to solve the awkward problems set by galleries, which here block a good part of the aisle windows.

* * *

Vanbrugh, Hawksmoor and Archer had a larger following than most English historians of architecture, with a bias against anything baroque, have been willing to allow. Sometimes their imitators were dilettanti like Aldrich. More often they belonged to the opposite end of the scale comprehended by the term architect in the wide sense it bore in the eighteenth century—to the class of men who were frequently employed to execute the designs of others but could also, when called on to do so, turn out a design themselves, and who may conveniently be called builder-architects.

William Smith of Warwick seems to have been a prominent member of this class at the beginning of the century. "Seems," because I cannot find positive proof that he actually designed a single building. He was one of the Messrs. Smith who, as noted, built the tower and nave of St. Mary's, Warwick, to Sir William Wilson's design. He also built Sutton Coldfield rectory; it is possible that Wilson, who lived in the neighbourhood, provided the design of this as well. And after Wilson's death William Smith rebuilt the parish church of Whitchurch, Shropshire.

In July, 1711, the fourteenth-century building at Whitchurch, Shropshire, followed the example of other churches about that time by suddenly collapsing. The foundation stone of the new church was laid in March, 1712, and the building consecrated in October 1713. Its total cost was £4,287 4s. 2d.; the money was raised partly by brief, partly by subscription—Whitchurch was on the road to Ireland, and among the subscribers were some prominent people—and partly by parish rate. The accounts are extant; the largest payment Smith received at any one time was over £3,400.[1] The new church (27) was, and remains, a fine

[1] Information kindly supplied by the Rector, the Rev. J. H. Hall, M.A.

building of its kind. Several of its external details, such as the niches and circular openings in the tower and the aprons below the nave cornice, may have been suggested by St. Philip's, Birmingham, although their handling has little of the vigour of Archer's work. The plan, too, is of the same general form, though with a simple apse for chancel and a nave of five bays instead of six ; a sixth bay to the west contains the entrance lobbies and gallery staircases flanking the tower, which projects slightly still further westward, and the south-west door is sheltered by a semi-circular porch. The nave arcades are carried on sandstone columns of the Tuscan order, while the apse, which is lit by three windows of the same pattern as those of the rest of the church, has a Corinthian pilaster order with full entablature over the pilasters and the cornice alone continued round the whole wall.

This treatment of the entablature in the apse recalls the south front of Stoneleigh Abbey, near Kenilworth, which was built (*c.*1720) by Francis Smith, who was presumably either a brother or a son of William Smith—and the rector of Whitchurch from 1707 until 1720 was Peter Leigh, no doubt a relation of Lord Leigh of Stoneleigh. It is generally stated that Francis Smith, who certainly designed Warwick Court House and Sutton Scarsdale, was architect as well as builder at Stoneleigh, but one learned authority[1] gives the design to Thomas Archer, and it is more than a little significant that Francis Smith appears to have been the builder of Umberslade Hall, which was the seat of the senior branch of the Archer family and is reasonably attributed to the same architect. There are other houses ascribed to " Smith of Warwick "; perhaps William, who in the past has been consistently overlooked, should take the credit for some of them. Confusion is worse confounded, however, by the fact that the parish church of Burton-on-Trent, as rebuilt 1719-26, is practically a reproduction of the one at Whitchurch. And here the builder or " undertaker ", as he is called in the vestry order-book, was Francis Smith. Did he copy his father's or brother's design of eight years before—or repeat his own ? Or was some third party the architect at Whitchurch ? The answer to these questions, which are typical of those confronting the student of eighteenth-century architecture at every turn, must await fresh knowledge.

A builder-architect who was influenced to some extent by Vanbrugh was John Price (d.1736). He is represented in the book of drawings at King's Weston discussed by Mr. Hussey in *English Homes*, where he is described as " of Wandsworth "; elsewhere he is " of Richmond ". The largest undertaking with which he is known to have been connected was the erection of Canons for the Duke of Chandos to the design of James Gibbs. Both Edward Shepherd and John James were also employed at Canons, but it would seem that the design as well as the erection of Little Stanmore church, of which all except the tower was rebuilt at the Duke's expense about 1714-5, may be attributed to Price. Outside it is not an elegant building. The plain pilasters and unmoulded window architraves of Vanbrugh's style become clumsy things in John Price's hands, just

[1] H. Muthesius, *Das Englische Haus.*

25 Whitchurch or Little Stanmore, Middlesex, 1714-15, probably by John Price

Paintings by Louis Laguerre

26 St. Mary, Warwick, 1694, by Sir William Wilson

27 Whitchurch, Shropshire, 1712-13

TWO TOWERS BUILT BY THE SMITHS OF WARWICK

as the steeple of St. Martin's-in-the-Fields became clumsy when John Price and his son Francis tried to adapt it for the church of St. George's, Southwark, twenty years later. Inside, there is more to hold the spectator; yet it is not Price's work but the *trompe l'oeil* decorations of Laguerre (25, 148, 149), for this is the church which is supposed to have inspired Pope's much quoted couplet. An account of the painter must be relegated to a later chapter ; here a bald list of his subjects at Little Stanmore will suffice. Over the altar at the east end is the Adoration of Jehovah ; north of the altar, the Holy Family ; south of it, the Deposition ; on the nave ceiling, Miracles ; on the north and south walls of the nave, Evangelists and Virtues ; in the central half-dome of the west gallery, or Chandos pew, the Ascension.

Price must have been a busy man in 1714. For besides his work at Stanmore he was engaged on two other churches. One of them, St. Mary-at-the-Walls, Colchester, was destroyed in the last century. But St. George's, Yarmouth, (23, 24) remains. It was built as a chapel of ease to the parish church, and the committee of trustees appointed to oversee the work stipulated that St. Clement Danes should be taken as model. Sir Reginald Blomfield pronounced in his airy way that the building erected " bears not the slightest resemblance " to Wren's church ; in point of fact the plan of the interior and the arrangement of the galleries—the practical aspects with which the trustees would naturally be most concerned—do follow St. Clement Danes very closely. The design of the steeple, too, surely derives from another work of Wren—the steeple of St. James, Garlickhithe. But the outsize pilasters around the nave, and the composition of doorway, window and pediment at the west end, are eloquent of Price's admiration for Vanbrugh's baroque.

The last architect to be mentioned in this chapter had a higher standing than either Smith or Price. The son of a parson, John James was a man of some learning. He translated books on architecture and gardening from both Italian and French, and he became Hawksmoor's fellow surveyor to the Commissioners appointed under the church-building act of 1711. Most of his work, of which St. George's, Hanover Square, is the best known example, lies within the present County of London. But St. Mary's, Twickenham, does not. It was designed in 1713 or 1714, the old church, with the exception of the tower, having fallen down in the earlier year. On plan James's church consists of an oblong nave ($65 \times 39\frac{1}{2}$ ft.) with a small chancel to the east and projections of three bays breaking forward slightly to north and south. Outside, the latter have pilasters running through their full height and are surmounted by triangular pediments. Built very substantially of brick with stone dressings, the church as a whole is dignified, masculine and unaffected, although the effect of the lofty interior is somewhat spoilt by the horizontal lines of the galleries, which have curious fronts after the pattern of a Doric frieze.

Chapter III

EARLY GEORGIAN (1714-1760)

THE most important group of churches dating from George I's reign are those built under the Act of Parliament of 1711 that provided for "fifty new churches in and about the Cities of London and Westminster and Suburbs thereof". It is notorious that the number of churches actually erected fell very far short of the number envisaged by the Act. As Sir Roger de Coverley said, "church work is slow", and Whig Latitudinarianism was not the ideal stepfather for a child of Tory Highchurchmanship, such as the Act was. However, for us there is consolation in the fact that the failure in quantity was amply made up in quality.

In terms of both quantity and quality, the greatest contribution to this London church-building movement was Nicholas Hawksmoor's. He designed six churches under the Act, and each is a masterpiece. Yet Hawksmoor's influence on subsequent church design was negligible. Partly this was because his personal style was too individual, and too intensely emotional, to invite or allow imitation. Even more it was because, by the time any of Hawksmoor's churches was as much as half built, a reaction against baroque architecture had already set in.

The style advanced by the opponents of baroque is commonly described as Palladian, the adjective having reference to its adherence to the principles and examples of the sixteenth-century Vicentine architect Andrea Palladio. An English translation of Palladio's *Quattro Libri dell' Architettura* was published by Giacomo Leoni in 1715-20, and the Earl of Burlington, whom contemporaries acknowledged to be the leader of the movement, followed up his sponsorship of William Kent's *Designs of Inigo Jones* (1727) with the publication in 1730 of Palladio's drawings of the restoration of the Roman *thermae* under the title *Fabbriche Antiche disegnate da Andrea Palladio*. Thus it is not surprising that the history of early Georgian architecture in general may be seen as the swift rise, followed by the unchallenged supremacy, of Palladianism. But there are not many English churches which can properly be called Palladian. The churches of the Italian master himself were not suitable prototypes, and the new fashion in church architecture, when it arrived, was set by an architect who was destined by training and temperament to stand outside the strict Palladian school—namely, James Gibbs.

* * *

In deference to chronology, three large pre-Gibbs churches must be discussed first. One of them, St. Modwen's, Burton-on-Trent, has already been mentioned. It is, as we have noted, practically a reproduction of

28 North Runcton, Norfolk, completed 1713, by Henry Bell of King's Lynn

29 Stoke Doyle, Northamptonshire, 1722-5

30 St. Paul, Sheffield, begun 1720, by Robert Platt of Rotherham
Demolished by the Corporation in 1929

31 Aynho, Northamptonshire, 1723 A country church in the Vanbrugh manner

St. Alkmund's, Whitchurch, and its builder was Francis Smith of Warwick. If it shows anything which the earlier church does not, it is the inadvisability, in copying another building, of departing from its design one tittle without a good reason for doing so. In this case the reason was not a good one ; it can only have been a desire to save money, with the result that Burton church, with its slightly lower and plainer nave and considerably lower and plainer tower, just fails to be the noble building that its Shropshire prototype is.

If there is a suspicion of Archer's style about the churches of Whitchurch and Burton-on-Trent, there was a deal more about St. Paul's, Sheffield, (30), which was demolished in 1929. There was enough, indeed, to lead to its sometimes being attributed to Archer. Actually its designer was George Platt, a Rotherham man, and the name of the builder was Wastenage. Of Platt little is discoverable. Born in 1699 or 1700, by trade he was a mason ; in 1731-3 he rebuilt the tower and part of the body of the church of Chapel-en-le-Frith, Derbyshire ; in 1743 he died. He also designed Wortley Hall, Yorkshire, but he cannot have supervised much of its erection, since the building operations did not begin until the year of his death.

The early history of St. Paul's, Sheffield, shows to what unfortunate results the rather haphazard eighteenth-century methods of providing extra church accommodation might lead. The population of Sheffield having far outgrown its parish church, in 1719 a goldsmith called Robert Downes offered £1,000 towards a new chapel of ease, plus £30 a year for a minister for it. Other subscribers came forward and in something under eighteen months the building was up and fit for use. Then the trouble began. For it was found that it had not been decided who was to have the right of presentation. Mr. Downes rather naturally felt that he had a perfectly good claim to it. But the patron of the parish church also claimed it, and so did the vicar. The dispute dragged on, causing, in the words of the Sheffield historian, John Hunter, " great heats and animosities, great disappointments to the subscribers, and great inconvenience to the inhabitants of Sheffield, who had the mortification of seeing a noble edifice raised for their accommodation standing year after year wholly unoccupied and useless ". The Archbishop of York was appealed to but was not helpful, and it was not until 1739, after Downes had taken the " strong measure " of licensing the building under the Act of Toleration as a meeting house for Protestant Dissenters, that things came to a head and Parliament passed an act enforcing a compromise solution. And so the church was finally opened in May, 1740, just under 20 years after the laying of the first stone. The dome was not added to the tower until 1769 and internal work in the chancel waited till 1772 for completion.

Holy Trinity, Leeds, another church of the early 'twenties, was also a chapel of ease in origin. Nor was its foundation unattended by difficulties, a local gentleman who had promised £1,000 failing to pay up when the time came. However, work began in 1721 and the building was completed six years later. The total cost was £4,563 9s. 6d., of which about four-fifths was raised by subscription and the rest by the sale of pews. The architect was William Halfpenny, author of a large number of builders' pattern-books of the kind which played so great a part in the dissemination of classical *motifs* in the Georgian epoch.

Halfpenny's improbable name, unlike that of the similar but better remembered—indeed unforgettable—Batty Langley, was of his own choosing. Really he was Michael Hoare, a Twickenham carpenter, and work of his is still to be seen as far from Leeds as Bristol. Holy Trinity, Leeds, is an oblong church of seven bays, with the base of the tower in the westernmost, and an apse. The nave is divided up with aisles by unfluted Corinthian columns of stone, standing on pew-height pedestals and supporting a continuous entablature on either side; the cornice alone of the entablature is continued round the apse. These massive colonnades, dominating the interior, mark a radical departure both from Wren's practice of raising the galleries on piers with a comparatively small order above, and from the arcaded scheme of such churches as St. Philip's, Birmingham. They represent, in fact, a Palladian solution of the problem, and Holy Trinity, whatever its faults, was a forward-looking design in its day. Its faults appear outside, where the south elevation, which fronts the street, has rather the appearance of an assemblage of features, carefully selected but not too skilfully composed, from one of Halfpenny's own pattern-books. By placing the smaller windows above the larger, Halfpenny departed from another Wren practice with none too happy effect, and by balancing the real door to the west with a false one to the east he produced a symmetry which contradicts the church's orientation. His original design for the steeple, as shown in his *Art of Sound Building*, was never carried out; the steeple actually built collapsed in 1839, to be succeeded by the present one, designed by R. D. Chantrell.

* * *

I have called the foregoing "pre-Gibbs churches", but the term needs qualification. Actually James Gibbs returned to England from Rome, where he had studied under the baroque architect Carlo Fontana, in 1708, and designed St. Mary-le-Strand in 1714. But St. Mary-le-Strand, remarkable building though it is, has not the historical significance of two of Gibbs's later churches, St. Martin's-in-the-Fields (1722-6) and All Saints', Derby (1723-5). And in any case what really made possible the Gibbs era of church design, as it might almost be called, was the publication of his *Book of Architecture*, containing measured drawings of his own executed works, and some unexecuted, in 1728. In its introduction Gibbs wrote: "What is here presented to the Public was undertaken at the instance of several Persons of Quality and others. . . . They were of opinion, that such a Work as this would be of use to such Gentlemen as might be concerned in Building, especially in the remote parts of the Country, where little or no assistance for designs can be procured." And this opinion was amply justified in the event. Gibbs's designs, transmitted through this handsome folio, had a great influence on English architecture; in the case of churches their influence lasted a hundred years.

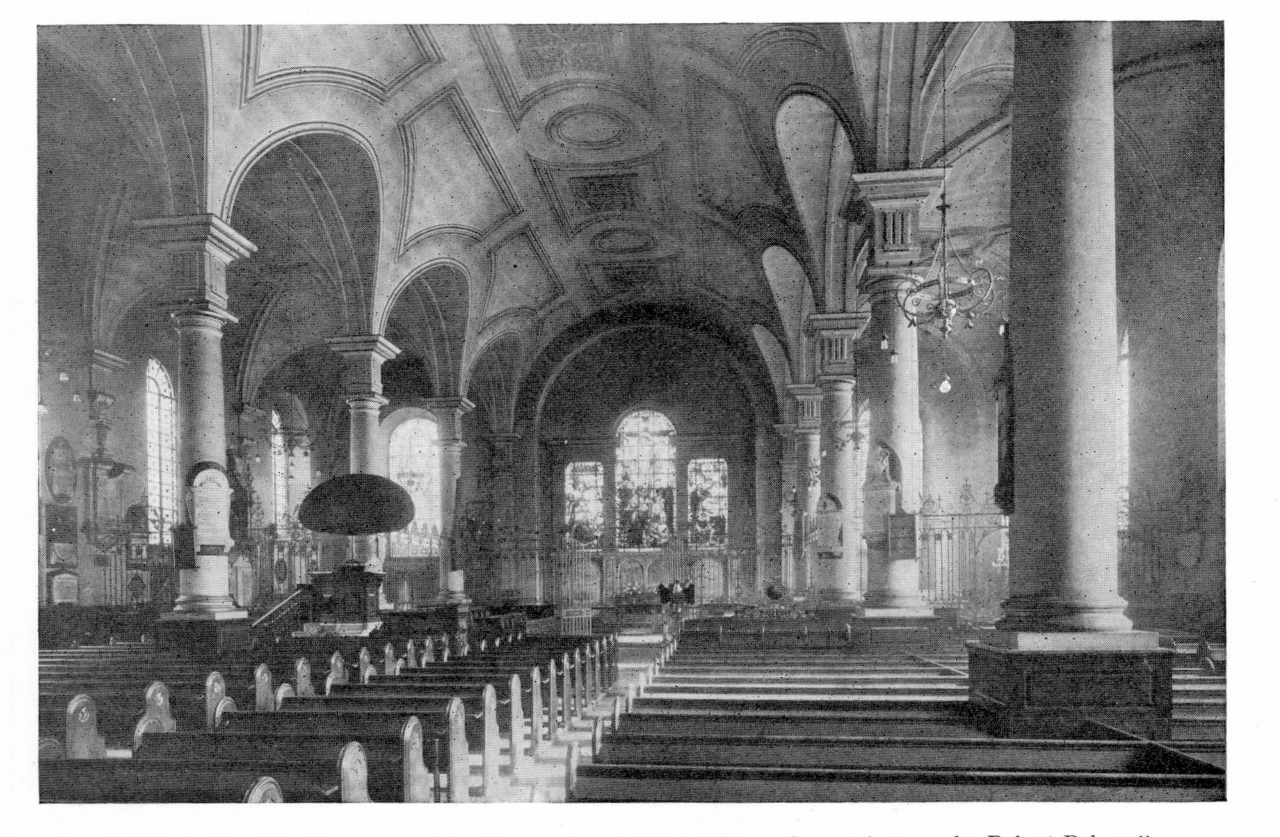

32 All Saints, Derby (now the cathedral), 1723-5, by James Gibbs Ironwork screen by Robert Bakewell

33 Honily, Warwickshire, 1723

34 St. John, Wolverhampton, 1755-60, by William Baker

35 St. Nicholas, Worcester, 1726-30, by Thomas White

Not everyone admired Gibbs's work, however. "No man talks of one edifice of Gibbs", wrote Horace Walpole, and his sweeping statement probably contained a measure of truth. For the taste of Walpole and his friends, when they were not amusing themselves with "the Gothick", was for the Palladianism of Lord Burlington's circle. And Gibbs, although he never broke a pediment out of doors, was no true Palladian. Indeed, how could the pupil of Fontana become such? But neither was he, except in one or two of his earliest buildings, a baroque architect. Gibbs's designs, in fact, show the national genius for compromise translated into architecture. And none more clearly than St. Martin's-in-the-Fields. In essentials this famous church is a combination of a Roman temple exterior, a high steeple, and a baroque interior. That, one might have thought, is compromise enough. But the spirit, or principle, or what you will, is carried right down into the component parts. Thus, as Mr. John Summerson has pointed out, "the heavy rustics of the windows constitute an academic solecism in a building ruled by the essentially feminine Corinthian order".[1] And then the steeple, which would appear at first sight to belong to the family of designs of which the steeples of St. Mary-le-Bow and St. Bride's are prominent members, is found on further inspection to ascend with a decorum which is utterly foreign to Wren's work. With its carefully differentiated storeys it represents, like the rest of the church, a compromise between baroque "licence" and Palladian "propriety".

It is too easy, perhaps, to damn Gibbs with faint praise. If he had not the genius of a Wren or a Hawksmoor, he was at any rate prodigiously talented. His work demands to be judged by the highest standards. And few of the buildings which lie within the scope of this book come out of the ordeal with such assurance as his Derby church.

The rebuilding of all but the fifteenth-century tower of All Saints', Derby, was attended by more than usually bitter disputes of the kind which make parochial history of the Georgian period more amusing than edifying. In 1719 a design was submitted by Francis Smith and he was asked to send in his estimate for carrying it out. But it was by no means a matter of general agreement that the church should be rebuilt at all, and when, in the autumn of 1722, a model of the proposed new church was produced for the inspection of the parishioners, the whole scheme aroused strong opposition. However, the leader of the party in favour of rebuilding was the minister, Dr. Hutchinson, who was not a man to be thwarted. A committee was chosen "to treate in all matters, relating to the New building this Church of All Sts." and within three months the redoubtable doctor had bullied his weaker opponents on it into apathy, and placated the rest by promising to hold himself personally responsible for the expenses of the new building, "under this single proviso, that they should not give his wife any molestation (for she was a woman that could not bear trouble) in case he dropped off before the work was finished". But before the chancel could be pulled down the consent of the Corporation, who held the advowson of All Saints', which was a Free

[1] *Georgian London, 1945*, pp.71-2.

Chapel outside diocesan control, had to be obtained, and the Corporation had from the first been the principal enemy to the rebuilding scheme. Nothing daunted, on February 18, 1722/3 before dawn, Dr. Hutchinson set on a gang of workmen to demolish the old fabric. Confronted thus with a *fait accompli* the Corporation determined to make the best of a bad job. One of the Aldermen was granted leave of absence to accompany Hutchinson on a tour to London, Oxford, Cambridge and other important towns in quest of subscriptions, and so successful were their combined efforts that they raised over £3,000.[1]

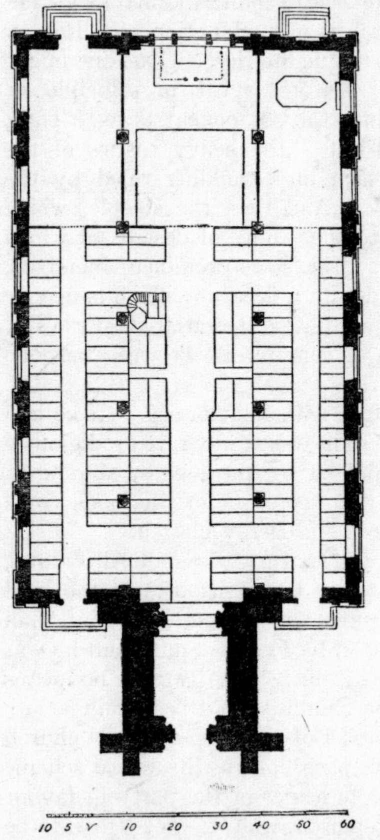

All Saints', Derby, 1723, by James Gibbs

The tale of Dr. Hutchinson's deeds and misdeeds does not end there, but we need not follow it further. Gibbs's design for All Saints' was adopted in preference to Smith's shortly before Hutchinson took the law with regard to the demolition of the chancel into his own hands. Francis Smith's services were retained as builder and he accomplished the work between May 1723 and November 1725. The total cost was £4,588 8s. 8d., a sum which includes £25 to Gibbs for his design and over half as much to the engraver Hulsbergh "for copper plate and 300 Cuts".

Gibbs himself was pleased with All Saints' (32). "It is the more beautiful," he wrote, "for having no Galleries, which, as well as Pews, clog up and spoil the Inside of Churches, and take away from that right Proportion which they otherwise would have, and are only justified as they are necessary." In this it differs from St. Martin's-in-the-Fields, and also in having no structural chancel, even internally. A feature it has in common with the London church is the device of interposing between the columns and the vaulting square slices of entablature. This device was not Gibbs's invention, and it has been severely criticized; the pontifical Fergusson thought that it was "perhaps the most fatal gift of Classic Art to modern times, as nine-tenths of the difficulties and clumsinesses of the revived Art are owing to the introduction of this feature". But as used by Gibbs in All Saints' it is surely justified,

[1] Sir Isaac Newton gave five guineas, Sir Robert Walpole twenty.

because it allowed him to keep both the proportions and the trappings of the Doric order and at the same time made possible a lightness, and a variety of diagonal vistas, which continuous entablatures, either from column to column or from each column to the outer wall of the aisle, would have prevented; the whole interior, instead of being cut up into three, is apprehended as a single space.

Compared with St. Martin's-in-the-Fields, rich with the plaster "fretwork" of Artari and Bagutti, the interior of All Saints' is cold. Ornament for ornament's sake is confined, almost, to the great wrought iron screens and gates (139), shutting off the sanctuary to the east, the mayor's parlour to the north, and the vestry to the south; these constitute the masterpiece of the Derby smith, Robert Bakewell. Gibbs wrote: "The plainness of this building makes it less expensive, and renders it more suitable to the old steeple." And beside the latter the exterior is modest, indeed self-effacing.

Two features shared by All Saints', Derby and St. Martin's-in-the-Fields, will crop up again and again in these pages. One is the slice of entablature over each column of the nave. The other is the blocked or rusticated architrave around windows and doors. This *motif* is common in English classical architecture of the eighteenth century. Wren never used it. Nor, although it is to be found in the work of the most doctrinaire of the Burlingtonian school, did Palladio; the Burlingtonians believed however, that they could point to precedents in the work of their other hero, Inigo Jones. It appears in the doorways of Halfpenny's church at Leeds, but Gibbs seems to have been the first to employ it for simple round-headed windows in series in the flanks of a church. No doubt it recommended itself to him as a means of emphasizing the openings without losing the general temple character at which he aimed; the alternative of small pediments over the windows, as seen in the Leeds church, belongs to the architecture of the palace rather than the temple. And Gibbs's use of the rusticated architrave set a fashion for church designers. It was easy to copy, and it offered a handy formula for giving consequence even to the simplest and smallest country church; thus we find it, for instance, at Biddlesden, Bucks. (*c.*1730), and, in cruder form, at Conington, Cambs. (1737). On a scale comparable to that of the churches in which Gibbs himself used it, it occurs at Gainsborough, Lincolnshire.

All Saints', Gainsborough, has, as a matter of fact, sometimes been attributed to Gibbs. But no documentary evidence exists, and most critics probably would agree with G. F. Bodley's view that it is not up to Gibbs's standard.[1] Nevertheless, it is good of its kind. As at Derby, the Gothic tower remains; the body of the church was rebuilt, largely with the proceeds of a special tax on coal brought into the town, in 1736-48. The lateral elevations resemble St. Martin's-in-the-Fields—for it is a galleried church—but with Doric pilasters instead of Corinthian. Inside, however, there are no specifically Gibbsian features. The Corinthian colonnades support unbroken entablatures running the length of the nave, and the interior in general recalls Holy Trinity, Leeds, being based on

[1] Quoted by C. Moor, *History of Gainsburgh* (Gainsborough, 1904). Bodley carried out internal work in the church in 1903.

the same system of proportions, although considerably larger; the continuation round the apse of the whole entablature, instead of the cornice alone, is a variation, in the direction of greater academic correctness, such as one would expect of the later date of the design. Was the

A pattern-book church with Gibbsian windows
(From John Aheron, *A General Treatise of Architecture*, Dublin 1759)

architect William Halfpenny? Or was he perhaps Francis Smith, whose contemporary rebuilding of the nave of Monmouth church evidently followed the same column-and-lintel principle? But by this time there were so many builder-architects who would have been capable of the design, with the assistance of the available pattern-books and of Gibbs's *Book of Architecture*, that such speculation is not very profitable.

* * *

An unexpected example of the influence of Gibbs's *Book of Architecture* on church design in the 1730's is provided by the steeple of St. Nicholas', Worcester (35), which is copied, with modifications, from one of the

36 St. Swithin, Worcester, 1733-6, by Edward and Thomas Woodward

37 Castle Bromwich, Warwickshire, 1726-31, probably by Thomas White

38 Gayhurst, Buckinghamshire, 1728

rejected designs for the steeple of St. Mary-le-Strand as published in that volume. It is the more surprising in that its architect, Thomas White, was by virtue of the style of the rest of his work a late survivor of the school of Wren.

White of Worcester may, indeed have worked for Wren, somewhere at some time. Nash's *Worcestershire* states that "Sir Christopher Wren took him to Rome [where of course Wren himself never went] and placed him with a statuary there", that "he by stealth made admeasurements of all the component parts of St. Peter's church, and assisted Sir Christopher in *modelling* that of St. Paul's, London," and that "Wren would have retained him for his foreman to superintend the building of St. Paul's". These are pretty fables; White's dates—he was born in 1673 or 1674 and died in 1748—show that they can be nothing more. They serve, however, to reinforce the probability of a White-Wren connection which is suggested by White's work.

An alternative design for the steeple of St. Mary-le-Strand published in Gibbs's *Book of Architecture* and adopted, with modifications, for St. Nicholas, Worcester (compare figure 35)

Primarily, White was a craftsman, a stone-carver. It was as a statuary that he described himself in his will, and the earliest documentary reference to him yet discovered, dated 1709, records that the Worcester City Chambers "ordered that Thomas White be and is admitted a Freeman of this City making a handsome effigie of the Queen to the well likeinge of the Mayor and Alderman for the time being but that he be not sworne before the Effigie be done". This statue of Queen Anne was later moved to a niche in the front of Worcester Guildhall. This, built in 1721-4, is White's earliest known work of architecture, and with its other statues, the great trophy in the central pediment, and the panels of sculptured ornament on the walls, is very much a stone-carver's building. The late survival of the mixed style of the seventeenth century in the architectural designs of such men as Thomas White may be explained by the fact that it was the craftsman's style *par excellence*. White was a mason-architect of the old tradition.

At least three churches may be attributed to White. Two of them are in his native city, and these shall be taken first. St. Nicholas' is the older, having been opened in 1730 (35). (But the steeple, whose provenance has been mentioned, is probably later.) All Saints' dates from 1738-42. It should be said at once that both churches are attributed to White solely on the word of tradition, as handed down by Nash; all that is known for certain is that the master-builders of All Saints' were Richard Squire and William Davis. But in this case tradition can reasonably be trusted.

The west end of St. Nicholas', at any rate, is patently by the architect of the Worcester Guildhall. It is surmounted by the same kind of segmental pediment, with the middle part cut back in the same way, and the pediment of the doorway is treated in similar fashion. The body of the church is severely plain—a spacious hall with a coved ceiling and an apse.

All Saints', White's other Worcester church, is a rather larger building. Unlike St. Nicholas' it is built on an aisled plan, with internal colonnades. Outside, the most notable features are the tower, a sturdy, masculine essay in the plainer Wren style, standing on a medieval substructure, and the baroque treatment of the short chancel, which has a huge east window, almost as high as the internal vault, flanked by Doric pilasters supporting portions of entablature and a pediment above. In the centre of the pediment—far too high to be seen properly—there is a bust, by White, of Bishop Hough, who was instrumental in getting All Saints' rebuilt.

A third Worcester Church which used to be attributed to White is St. Swithin's (1734-6). But the researches of Mr. Howard Colvin have now revealed that St. Swithin's was not only built, but also designed, by the Chipping Campden masons, Edward and Thomas Woodward. Here, as at St. Nicholas', architectural effect is necessarily concentrated at one end, but this time it is the east. The designers were confronted, in fact, with the classic problem with which Inigo Jones at Covent Garden, for example, and Hawksmoor at Greenwich had been confronted—how to combine eastern entrances with an eastern altar; they solved it by screening the chancel from the vestibules on either side by oak panelled walls about 8 feet high supporting columns which rise to the roof. The interior of St. Swithin's (36) is as a whole delightful. It retains practically all its original fittings, including a very grand pulpit, and it is covered by a plaster ceiling of shallow segmental section which with its system of transverse and diagonal ribs looks forward to the "rococo Gothic" of subsequent decades.

We return to White with the parish church of Castle Bromwich, Warwickshire (37). This is an interesting building in more than one respect. Until 1726 a medieval church of timber occupied the site. In that year Sir John Bridgeman, Bart., whose house stood within a couple of hundred yards of the church, decided on something more modern. There can be no doubt but that White was Bridgeman's architect; he had already employed him as a monumental sculptor, and the new church, which was completed by 1731, has a number of tell-tale details. The fluted aprons under the windows, their elaborately moulded architraves, the oblong and oval panels on the walls and parapet, the curved pediment-like features over the porches—all these can be paralleled in White's Worcester buildings and are typical of the highly-wrought, slightly *bizarre* style of this follower of Wren, who was first and last a mason even

39 Redlands Green Chapel, Bristol, 1743, by John Strachan: the west end

40 St. Thomas, Stourbridge, Worcestershire, 1726: the interior, looking east The Chancel was added in 1890

41 Mereworth, Kent, 1744-6 With a steeple after St. Martin-in-the-Fields

42 First Baptist Meeting House, Providence, Rhode Island, U.S.A., 1775, by Joseph Brown The steeple reproduces one of the rejected designs for St. Martin-in-the-Fields

when, as here, his main structural material was brick. But the oddest point about Castle Bromwich church is yet to be mentioned; the old wooden church was not pulled down but was *encased* in the new building. This fact accounts for much that is strange in the proportions of the latter, and also for the flatness of the internal arches, which, with their supporting columns, are mere plaster shells concealing the posts and beams of the earlier structure.

Thomas White is representative of a large class; the architecture of our provincial towns shows that there were many men of similar status and talents. But in too many cases we do not know even their names. Who designed St. Thomas's, Stourbridge for example? (40). It is exactly contemporary with Castle Bromwich church and was built by subscription, the inhabitants of the growing town of Stourbridge having wearied of the walk to their parish church at Old Swinford. The only surviving document which names anyone employed in its erection would seem to be "an accot. of Bricks Laid by S. Parker" (61,500 at 2s. 6d. per thousand). It may be significant that a Thomas Parker, mason, helped to build the Meeting House at Stourbridge in 1698.[1] The Parkers *may* have been the Stourbridge counterparts of White of Worcester and the Smiths of Warwick. Or they may have been simple tradesmen. But questions of authorship apart, St. Thomas's, Stourbridge, with its well managed vaulting (which follows the general scheme of St. James's, Piccadilly), is an attractive building. More so, perhaps, than the two years older St. Edmund's in the neighbouring town of Dudley—which has, however, some interesting baroque detail at the west end, and points in common with the churches built by the Smiths at Whitchurch and Burton.

St. Thomas's, Stourbridge, 1726, before the addition of the present chancel in 1890
From an early nineteenth-century engraving

The Bastards of Blandford are among the minority of provincial builder-architects of this period whose names have come down to us. Blandford was one of the phœnix towns of the eighteenth century. The

[1] For this information and a copy of the bricklaying account, I am indebted to Alderman H. E. Palfrey, F.S.A.

fire by which it was consumed, to rise again in greater splendour, took place in 1731. The builder responsible for much of the new town was John Bastard; his brother Thomas died in the year of the fire. The case of the Bastards is more than a little like that of the Smiths of Warwick. For they too, it would seem, had probably worked for Thomas Archer. Examination of all the evidence for supposing that this was so would take us far from our present subject, but it may be noted that at some date prior to 1720 Archer moved to Hale (not twenty miles from Blandford) where he built himself a house which shows, incidentally, that even he was not impervious to Palladian ideas.

Whatever connection may have existed between the two men, and whether or not Archer overlooked and corrected John Bastard's design, the church which the latter built at Blandford between the fire and 1739 belongs rather to the Wren-baroque tradition than to any newer school (46). Even if it is not a masterpiece, it is one of the more remarkable English churches of its time. A criticism which has been levelled at it is that the tower is too slender for the body of the church. The great pedimented porches to the north and south of the nave are a notable feature; their internal effect, unhappily, is spoilt by the galleries, installed later in the eighteenth century. It will be remembered that John James had made play with lateral pediments at Twickenham; and so had Archer at Deptford. More than anything else, in fact, these porches help to "place" Bastard's design. For they introduce a north-south axis which marks Blandford church as fundamentally different in conception from the large church of Gibbs and his imitators, which, aspiring to the condition of a classical temple, is planned about a single axis running east and west.

* * *

The churches discussed at any length in this chapter so far have all been town churches—except Castle Bromwich, which has the plan and dimensions of one. The time has come to retrace our steps and glance at a few of the country churches begun between 1714 and 1740. By way of preface it should be pointed out that nearly every rebuilt country church of the Georgian era is smaller than the former church on its site was; intended exclusively for worship on Sundays and kept locked every other day of the week, it was designed to fit its congregation and did not have the fulfil the multifarious functions for which its medieval predecessor was built. It should also be noted that many country churches were erected at the expense of one man, the lord of the manor; and among these are the most interesting, since the lord of the manor, as a person of taste, was more likely to be concerned with the appearance of the new building and to employ an architect than the average parish vestry. But to trace the designers of such churches is always difficult, and often impossible. Vestry books and churchwarden's accounts do not help, and where family papers are not forthcoming there is generally nothing except the uncertain evidence of style to show who may have been responsible.

43 Stoke Edith, Herefordshire, 1740

44 Mereworth, Kent, 1744-6

TWO DORIC INTERIORS

45 Daventry, Northamptonshire, 1752, by William and David Hiorn

46 Blandford, Dorset, 1731-9, by John Bastard

However, it seems pretty certain that the 1715 rebuilding of all but the tower of the little church of Charlton Marshall, Dorset, was the work of one of the Bastards, or, as is perhaps more likely, of the family working in partnership as country builders. Evidently he, or they, had not yet fallen under the spell of Thomas Archer, as it seems that John, at any rate, later did. For the delights of Charlton Marshall church, with its walls of chequered flint and stonework, are those of texture and craftsmanship, and not strictly architectural, while the stepped buttresses set diagonally at the eastern angles of the nave hark back to Gothic practice. But who can have been responsible for Tyberton church, Herefordshire? This dates from 1720. Outside it is ordinary enough, a red brick structure with a west tower and nave and chancel under separate roofs. But within it has an apsidal sanctuary covered by a half-dome and lined with oak, while the panels which should contain the Creed and Commandments are framed with high relief carvings among whose subjects are the Emblems of the Passion—symbolism little expected from the reign of George I.

Among the churches of the 'twenties which one would most wish to have seen was that of Shipbourne, Kent, which was designed by James Gibbs in 1721 (52). But it was demolished in a Gothic rage in 1880, and for its appearance we have to rely on a drawing in the Maidstone museum, which shows it to have been a simple oblong building with an unbroken roof line and a tower, crowned by urns and a cupola, rising from the centre of the westernmost bay.

The church at Hale, which is attributed to Thomas Archer, also suffered in Victorian days, although not to the point of destruction; the altered windows and roof make it hard to judge of its original qualities. There are other notable county churches belonging to the Wren-baroque movement at Stoke Doyle (29, 118) and Aynho (31), Northamptonshire, and Honily (33), Warwickshire. Stoke Doyle was begun in 1722; its most striking external feature is the south door with its segmental pediment and bold rustication. Both the others were begun in 1723. Aynho, which retains a medieval tower, is a fairly large hall-type church, with extremely domestic-looking side elevations of two storeys; the influence of Vanbrugh is patent. Honily (33), on the other hand, is very small, almost a toy church, but it is treated with much architectural circumstance. Approached between ball-topped gate piers, it has a massive tower surmounted by a short spire, while the interior is adorned with Corinthian columns supporting the west gallery and Corinthian pilasters in the apse.

The designers of Stoke Doyle, Honily and Aynho churches are not known. But stylistic evidence, coupled with considerations of geography, enable us to make a shrewd guess in the latter two cases. The architect at Honily may well have been Francis Smith; Aynho was very likely designed and built by the Oxford mason William Townesend, who had worked for both Aldrich and Hawksmoor and possibly for Vanbrugh too. The church at Gayhurst, Bucks, presents a more difficult problem (38). There is indeed a local Wren tradition, and it is sometimes described as Wren's last building. But there seems to be no supporting evidence. The faculty to take down the old church was granted in 1724, the year of Wren's death ; the new one was begun in 1728. Whoever designed it, Gayhurst church is a fascinating building, both for its architectural qualities and, historically, as an exceptionally complete example of a church of its time, preserving nearly all its original fittings intact. Outside, the treatment of the south side of the nave, with its Ionic order raised on a rusticated plinth, its central doorway with shouldered architrave and semicircular pediment, and the triangular pediment forcing forward from the main line of the eaves, is distinctly baroque, although more delicate in detail than the " heroic baroque " of Vanbrugh and his followers. The little cupola has a kind of fancifulness which accords curiously well with the early seventeenth-century house by which the church stands ; it might almost be one of those " shapes " (as they were called) which crowned the many turrets of the larger Elizabethan and Jacobean mansions, although it is hardly to be supposed that the Georgian designer of the church intended any such allusion. Within, there is much good plasterwork and joinery, including an oak reredos of a type found in Wren's London churches.

Biddlesden and Conington churches, both dating from the 'thirties, have already been mentioned as showing the influence of Gibbs. Neither is specially notable in itself, although Biddlesden has some good fittings. But the parish church of Great Witley, Worcestershire (49, 144, 150, 153), is quite another matter. It has, in fact, about the most sumptuous example of a full-blown rococo interior in England.

Witley church was built at the expense of the widow of the first Lord Foley and opened in 1735. It was then a quite plain structure of brick with stone dressings and the cupola which it still bears ; the walls themselves were not faced with stone until a century and a quarter later. The architect is unknown ; evidently he was an admirer of Gibbs, if he was not Gibbs himself. Nor is anything known of the original appearance of the church internally. For the ceiling paintings which now adorn it, and the painted glass which fills the windows, cannot have been inserted before 1747, when they were purchased by the second Lord Foley at the sale of the contents of Canons, the palace of the " magnificent " Duke of Chandos, Pope's Timon, who has already figured in these pages as the builder of Little Stanmore church. There they adorned the Duke's private chapel, having been executed in 1719-21, the glass by Joshua Price after designs by Sebastiano Ricci, and the ceilings probably by Antonio Bellucci; the splendid gilt plasterwork is of doubtful authorship, the most likely candidate for the distinction of having created it being Bagutti. We shall consider these artists in a later chapter ; at Witley their respective contributions harmonize perfectly, to produce an *ensemble* which is one of the triumphs of the Georgian decorative arts—and the most unlikely of settings for the Anglican liturgy.

* * *

During the period 1740-60 incomparably the most important single influence in English church architecture was that of Gibbs. Gibbs himself lived until 1754, but the latest building of his with which we are concerned here, Patshull church, Staffordshire (119), was built some twelve years before his death. It is a straightforward common-sense design; an adaptation of the contemporary classicism to the traditional form of the English country church. Unlike the same architect's Shipbourne church of twenty years earlier, it has a structural chancel which is clearly differentiated inside and out, although Gibbs has varied the roof levels as little as may be. The tower, too, abuts the west wall of the church instead of rising from the last bay; its upper part (to judge from the engraving in Stebbing Shaw's *Staffordshire*) has been rebuilt to an altered design in comparatively recent times.

Of all Gibbs's buildings, the most frequently imitated was St. Martin's-in-the-Fields. Its popularity as a model was due to a number of causes, among which are to be reckoned the wide applicability of its plan, the attractiveness of its style of architecture—which was, as has been suggested, rather more ornamental than that of the strict Palladian school and a good deal less emotional than the baroque of Hawksmoor—and, as much as anything, the general accessibility of the design in Gibbs's *Book of Architecture*. There may too, one suspects, sometimes have been an element of snobbery at work; for St. Martin's was a church, not of the plebeian City, but of aristocratic Westminster, and it had been extremely costly to build.

The most original (and most questionable) feature of St. Martin's, the placing of the steeple over the roof and immediately behind the deep prostyle portico, was not, at first, often copied; for an example from the first half of the eighteenth century we should have to go as far afield as Glasgow.[1] But the steeple itself was a frequent model, the earliest and most famous imitation of it being the steeple of Henry Flitcroft's St. Giles's-in-the-Fields.

The Steeple of St. Giles's-in-the-Fields, Henry Flitcroft, architect
The lower stages served as a model for Daventry steeple (compare figure 45)

To understand how one architect could borrow so elaborate a feature from the building of another, without any attempt at concealment and

[1] St. Andrew's, 1739-55; architect, Allan Dreghorn.

without his contemporaries thinking any the worse of him for it, we must remember that the aim of classical art is not expression but perfection—the attainment of ideal beauty rather than the manifestation of unique personality. It follows from this that when classical theories of art obtain, imitation really is felt to be the sincerest form of flattery. It also follows that any particular design can almost certainly be "improved". And this, in fact, is what Flitcroft tried to do to St. Martin's steeple; his version at St. Giles's shows certain deviations from the original, small but significant and all tending to greater "correctness" as that true Palladian, "Burlington Harry", understood the term.

In looking at eighteenth-century architecture we do well to keep the implications of classical art theory in mind; much that would otherwise seem mere plagiarism is then explained. But surely the copy of St. Martin's steeple that perches rather self-consciously on the church at Mereworth, Kent (41, 44), owes its presence there to nothing more recondite than the strong collecting instinct which caused spurious Raphaels and fake Titians to embrown the walls of so many Georgian mansions. Mereworth church was built in 1744-6 at the expense of the seventh Earl of Westmoreland; its architect is not known. Horace Walpole in 1752 described it as "a new church with a steeple which seems designed for the latitude of Cheapside, and is so tall that the poor church curtsies under it, like Mary Rich in a vast high-crown hat". And it must be confessed that the Tuscan "barn" which constitutes the body of Mereworth church is rather overpowered by Gibbs's ornate steeple. In itself, with its deep spreading eaves and semicircular porch, it represents a purer classicism than is found in most churches of its age. The interior, with a barrel vault over the nave and flat ceilings to the aisles, is of a type common enough in simplified form. But here, in addition to the colonnades supporting the vault, an outer colonnade runs round the walls, and the whole has the air of being a careful and learned reconstruction of some building of classical antiquity. The columns are painted in imitation of marble and the ceilings in imitation of stone coffering, while the details of the entablature also are the work of the brush and not of the chisel. "The most abominable piece of tawdriness", Walpole thought it all, but since he wrote the colours have faded, to produce exquisite combinations of cool pinks, greys, and browns.

The hand of the amateur—perhaps the noble amateur—is surely to be detected in the design of Mereworth church. But St. John's, Wolverhampton (34), is the work of a builder architect, William Baker.[1] It was begun in 1755, and from the plan to the design of the steeple it owes everything to Gibbs and nearly everything to St. Martin's; outside, at any rate, it is practically a reproduction of that famous church, though reduced in size and denuded of portico and pilasters. Even if it is not strikingly original, it cannot be denied that it dominates the square in which it stands in a handsome manner, and one can imagine that to the Wolverhampton parishioners who built it as a chapel of ease it must have seemed very grand indeed.

[1] Information from Mr. Howard Colvin.

47 Daventry, Northamptonshire, 1752 by William and David Hiorn

48 St. Philip, Birmingham (now the cathedral), 1709-15, by Thomas Archer: the interior before the addition of the present chancel
From an early nineteenth century engraving

49 Great Witley, Worcestershire, 1735, with stucco-work and paintings by Antonio Bellucci installed in or after 1747. From an early nineteenth century drawing in the possession of Mr. Paul Foley

As we have seen in the case of St. Nicholas', Worcester, (35) it was not only Gibbs's executed designs that found imitators. And sometimes the imitator became the imitated. When the brothers William and David Hiorn, who had by this time succeeded the Smiths as the most important builder-architects of Warwick, were called on to design a new church for Daventry, they hit on the labour-saving device of copying the steeple of St. Giles's-in-the-Fields, omitting the octagon above the clock stage and substituting for Flitcroft's a spire taken from one of the alternative designs for the steeple of St. Martin's as shown in Gibbs's book. The result is hardly elegant, and it is with a rather gouty Georgian finger that Daventry church points the way to Heaven (45). Its nave combines the vaulting plan and Doric order of All Saints', Derby, with the galleried arrangement of St. Martin's ; the columns, it may be noted, are wooden shells, plastered in imitation of stone, with octagonal pillars of real stone inside (47).

The Hiorns were capable of better things than Daventry church which dates from 1752. One of them was St. Bartholomew's, Birmingham, begun three years earlier. Unfortunately this church, which had been disused for some years before the war, was destroyed in an air-raid. It was a galleried building with two ranges of windows and no tower but a cupola at one end—somewhat after the pattern of Gibbs's St. Peter's, Vere Street, in fact.

Of course not every church, not even every large church, was based on Gibbsian models during this period. A great many were built in an unpretentious style which without any intent to defame we may christen Carpenter's Classical. St. Peter's, Congleton, is a plain example dating from 1742 which preserves most of its original fittings ; its Gothic tower was added in 1786. Another Cheshire church, that of Knutsford, (1744)(57) represents a more ornamental version of the style, with stone parapet and window dressings and a doorway which looks as though it had been taken direct from some contemporary pattern-book. Holy Trinity, Guildford (begun 1749) is a large-ish home counties specimen, and the coeval St. Julian's, Shrewsbury, may also be included in the category ; the architect of the latter church was Thomas Farnolds Pritchard (d. 1777), who is of interest chiefly as the designer of the first cast-iron bridge ever erected in England, which was made at the Coalbrookdale works and still spans the Severn at Ironbridge. All these are brick buildings, and Carpenter's Classical was over a great part of England necessarily a brick style. But the church of Helston, Cornwall, which, as recorded on the brass chandelier that is its chief ornament, was the " sole gift and benefaction of the Right Honorable the Earl of Godolphin ", is stone-built ; the nave was begun in 1756 to the design of Bland of Truro, while the later tower is by one Edwards.

* * *

When all is said, it is often the smaller country church that most repays the seeking out. Even when its architecture is of no exceptional distinction it sometimes retains furniture and fittings which Victorian vestries, with money to burn, cast out of its larger urban contemporary long ago. At Wheatfield, Oxon (50, 51), there is a little church with much that is pleasant of this kind, including a particularly handsome communion table (137) and some Georgian painted glass. The actual walls of Wheatfield church are medieval, but it was remodelled with Venetian window and classical porch in 1740 and has scarcely been touched since. The nave of Stoke Edith church, Herefordshire (43), on the other hand, was completely and substantially rebuilt in that year in the form of a plain hall with Doric columns screening the sanctuary at the east end and a gallery at the west. This is a building with some pretensions to style, although its designer got into trouble with his Doric order and was driven to the expedient—rather shocking from an academic point of view—of varying the spacing of his triglyphs to make it fit. Few churches of this class can be attributed to the better known architects of the day. Wimpole, Cambridgeshire, however, has one by Henry Flitcroft, dating from 1749; it was horribly treated in 1887, and a fine reredos is now about the only original fitting left. Many of these smaller churches have some sort of bellcote instead of a tower, although the English passion for tower-building was of course indulged in at this time as at every other. Occasionally steeples of the Wren-Gibbs genus were attempted; Great Houghton, near Northampton (79), for example, has a specimen dating from 1754, in which the tower is surmounted by a feature with a peristyle of eight free-standing columns and a short spire above.

Rejected design for the steeple of St. Martin's-in-the-Fields in Gibbs's *Book of Architecture* (1728), used by Joseph Brown for a church at Providence, Rhode Island, U.S.A., in 1775 (42)

Of all the small churches of the mid-century, that of Redlands Green, Bristol (39, 53)—suburban now, but rural when it was opened in 1743—is perhaps the most remarkable. Its west elevation is dressed up with an engaged portico in which one may detect a reminiscence of Vanbrugh's King's Weston; somewhat Vanbrugian too, or at any rate baroque rather than Palladian, is the central composition of doorway and niche above. But the cupola has a flavour all its own, and is as good as can be. Nothing could be simpler, or more decorative, than the way its architect has contrived the transition from the square to the octagon, and the ribbed, umbrella-like dome has just the festive quality the rest of the design demands. Inside, there is some superb carved woodwork, in a belated Grinling Gibbons manner; architecturally, again something

50 Exterior from the south-east

51 Interior looking east

Wheatfield, Oxfordshire A medieval church modernised in 1740

52 Shipbourne, Kent, 1722, by James Gibbs Demolished in 1880
From a drawing in the Maidstone Museum

53 Redlands Green Chapel, Bristol, 1743, by John Strachan

of Vanbrugh's boldness in the treatment of the entablature round the sanctuary and in the arched composition screening the entry—and helping to support the cupola—at the west end. John Strachan, who designed this delightful building, came to Bristol about 1726, and in the next ten years was responsible for a large number of houses in Bath. It is hard to believe that anyone else could have been the architect of the little church at Babington, Somerset (55), which, built in 1750, is in many respects a simpler version of Redlands Green, and quite as charming in its quieter way.

Strachan belongs to that west country galaxy of talent in which the elder John Wood's star shines brightest across the years. And so, perhaps, although here he was possibly working to the design of the amateur architect Thomas Prowse, did the builder who in 1751 raised the octagonal dome of Berkeley church, near Frome (54), with a mention of whose delicate rococo plasterwork this chapter may close.

NOTE.—A vulgar error derives the typical American church of the eighteenth century from Wren prototypes. In point of fact, the influence at work was that of Gibbs, and it crossed the Atlantic in *A Book of Architecture*. A classic example in proof of this is provided by the First Baptist Meeting House, Providence, Rhode Island (42) (1775, Joseph Brown, architect), the steeple of which is copied from one of the six "alternative draughts" for the steeple of St. Martin's. Other notable American churches inspired by Gibbs include the First Congregational Church, Providence; St. Michael's, Charleston, South Carolina; Congregational Church, Middleburg, Vermont; St. Paul's Chapel, New York City. One Virginian architect—John Ariss—actually advertised in 1751 that he would undertake buildings in the style of Gibbs ("either of the Ancient or Modern Order of Gibbs' Architect").

Mistley Church, Essex, 1766, by Robert Adam
Body of church demolished 1870

Chapter IV

LATER GEORGIAN (1760-1811)

By 1760, English architecture was ready for a change. Since the publication of Leoni's edition of Palladio, Kent's *Designs of Inigo Jones*, and Gibbs's *Book of Architecture*, a new generation of architects had grown up. Some sort of revolt against the accepted authorities of the reigns of the first two Georges was in the nature of things inevitable, and increased knowledge of classical antiquity provided its leaders with the necessary weapons. The general characteristics of the style which resulted, its elegance and refinement, are well known. Its essential differences from what had gone before were described by its most celebrated practitioner as "a remarkable improvement in the form convenience, arrangement, and relief of apartments; a greater movement and variety in the outside composition, and in the decoration of its inside, an almost total change".

Robert Adam, when he wrote the preface to his *Works in Architecture* was not thinking of churches. But many of the churches of the age do nevertheless, exhibit the same characteristics—the same use of curved and concave shapes in internal planning, similar picturesque grouping externally, and, needless to say, the same kind of ornament. We may feel that, in the case of churches at any rate, the new tendencies wer

54 Berkeley, Somerset, 1751: the dome, with rococo plasterwork of the West Country school

55 Babington, Somerset, 1750

not at all such unmixed blessings as Adam, with understandable partiality, represented them. The shifting of interest from the structural elements of classical design to purely decorative *motifs* was apt to result in a certain emptiness. William Halfpenny was no great architect, but the interior of Holy Trinity, Leeds, has a kind of dignity which is not shared by many churches of George III's reign. Church design was growing more secular, as it were; tastefulness and commodiousness were sought, sometimes to the detriment of other qualities which we may feel to be more important. On the other hand, the new interest in "space composition" produced some remarkable churches with plans of more concentrated forms than the basilican type practically universal between 1720 and 1760.

* * *

Robert Adam's church at Laswade, near Edinburgh, planned as a Greek cross containing a rotunda, and his design for the church in Charlotte Square in that city, which was much altered in execution by Robert Reid after Adam's death, do not belong to our subject. But they may be mentioned in passing, because they suggest that Adam, given the chance, might have made as important a contribution in this sphere as in domestic architecture. His opportunities, however, were few. He made a design for the rebuilding of the church at Wonersh, Surrey, but this was not carried out; at Gunton Park, Norfolk, he built, in 1769, a small church of white brick with a Doric portico. The church of Mistley, Essex, was a more important work. Here Adam was called in, in 1766, to "give tone" (as a later age would have put it) to a plain brick building of 1735. This he did by adding a tower at either end—

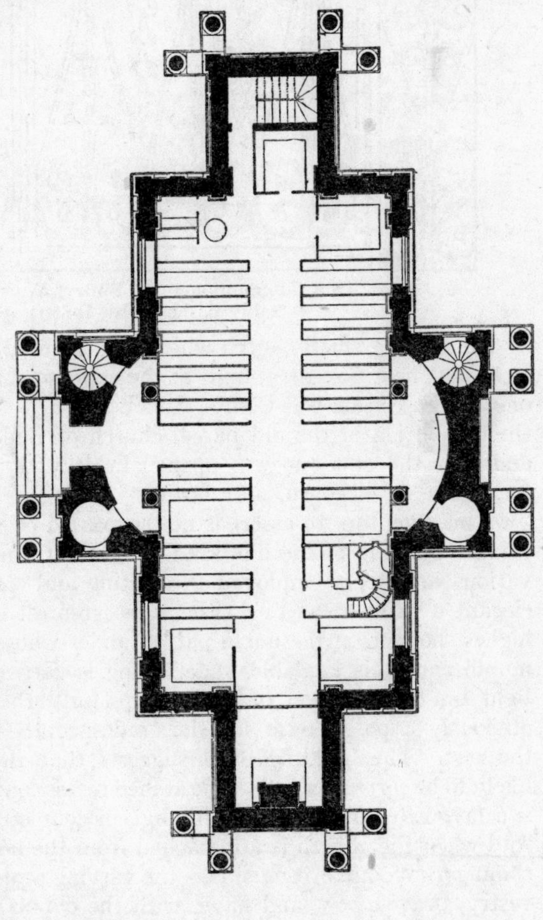

Mistley church, Essex, 1766, by Robert Adam

the base of that to the east containing the chancel—while in the middle of its flanks he built out porticoed projections which gave, internally, shallow segmental recesses screened by Ionic columns and furnished with galleries. The result was quite unlike any previous English church. Unfortunately the body of it was demolished in 1870, and the towers alone, made symmetrical by the addition of columns from the destroyed porticos, were left standing—to serve, it is said, as a navigation mark or craft on the river Stour.

Iron Communion rails, Binley, Warwickshire, possibly designed by Robert Adam

An existing small church which is attributed to Robert Adam is that at Binley, near Coventry, built at the expense of the sixth Earl of Craven, one of whose seats was Combe Abbey nearby. The registers record that the demolition of the old parish church of Binley began in June, 1771, and that the new one was opened in July, 1773. " This noble fabric for neatness, elegance, and beauty ", says the contemporary account, " we may venture to assert is not surpassed or scarcely equalled by any private building of the like kind in the kingdom, and is finished by the various architects employed in erecting and completing the same in so elegant a manner, as to do them the greatest credit and to reflect the highest honour on the noble patron under whose auspices and by whose munificence this laudable undertaking is carried on." This throws no light on the question of authorship, for " the various architects " is obviously a polite term for the tradespeople—masons, plasterers, and the rest. The building itself suggests that the Adam tradition is as likely to be correct as not. The arched recess containing the west doorway is a favourite Adam device although of course not peculiar to his work. And when the church is approached from the north-east—as, by anyone coming from Combe, it must be—the varying projections and roof levels of vestry, Craven pew, and nave, with the cupola behind, have just " the rise and fall, the advance and recess, with other diversity of forms " that are comprised in Adam's definition of the quality of " movement ".

But most of all it is the charming green and white interior, with its divisions marked by open screens of alabaster columns, that lends support to the traditional attribution (64). The east window, a Holy Family painted almost entirely in enamels, is by William Peckitt of York.

Adam's rival, James Wyatt, was applied to for a design for St. Chad's, Shrewsbury, but characteristic dilatoriness lost him this opportunity. He did, however build several churches, including Hafod, Cardiganshire, Hanworth, Middlesex, East Grinstead, Sussex (a new Gothic nave), St. Peter's, Manchester, and Dodington, Gloucestershire. Time has dealt hardly with more than one of them, and St. Peter's, Manchester, which sounds a particularly attractive building, was completely demolished in 1907. It was opened in 1794, having been built by subscription; in the words of a Regency guide-book, " the subscribers had the good sense to reject the old rules which had not utility for their object, and dared to introduce comfort, convenience and propriety into the temple of God ". The design was symmetrical about either axis and there were two Doric porticos, one of which, with the new consciousness of the demands of town planning, was designed to " terminate the prospect " down Mosley Street. According to the authority already quoted, " the architect wished, instead of a steeple, to have preserved the Grecian order in its purity, by erecting a dome. In this measure he was overruled, and he designed a beautiful steeple, as much in unison with the rest of the building as possible ". But no steeple was built at first, and it was left to the prolific Francis Goodwin, architect of the old Manchester Town Hall, to add one after Wyatt's death.

Wyatt's most successful design in this department, however, is without doubt the little church at Dodington, built in 1805 (103). It was designed and built as the private Chapel of the House (now a School) and has later been created the parish church. Planned as a Greek cross with four barrel vaults and a coffered dome in the centre, it has a crystalline purity of form which is rare in English architecture.

John Carr of York, a provincial architect with something more than a local reputation, both in his lifetime and after, has been called a " late Burlingtonian ". Certainly much of his domestic work is in the manner of the earlier part of the century. But he had come into contact with Robert Adam over Harewood House, and as the most widely employed architect in Yorkshire he had to keep abreast of the fashion. Thus the stone-built church which he presented to his native village of Horbury in 1791 has next to nothing about it of Inigo Jones or Palladio, but a good deal of Adam.

Horbury Church (63) is said to have cost Carr £8,000—a sum which he could well afford, since when he died in 1807 he left £150,000, a fortune exceeded among those of professional architects of George III's reign only by Sir Robert Taylor's £180,000. It is fairly large as churches of the time go. The central area of the nave is a double square of sixty feet by thirty on plan, with a segmental ceiling. At either end is a shallow apse as wide as the nave, that to the west containing the organ in a gallery. To north and south are what are better described as porches than as aisles, each screened by two Corinthian columns supporting the main entablature, which is carried round the rest of the interior on pilasters. Outside, the south porch, which faces the village (although it does not lie on the axis of any street) is dressed up with engaged Ionic columns and a pediment; at the west end—or, having regard to the portico, should one say "on the west side"?—is a steeple of diminishing stages with a spire at the top. The apses are not expressed in the design of the exterior, but each is enclosed within three sides of an octagon. T. D. Whitaker in his *History of Leeds* (1816) was outspoken in criticism of this peculiarity, which he thought resulted in "a kind of anomalous termination utterly unknown to antiquity", and also of the placing of the steeple, which he thought should stand separate from the body of the church. "On the whole", he sums up, "I am sorry to say that the exterior of this elaborate building presents nothing to the eye but a beautiful and majestic portico misplaced." And Carr's church has, indeed, the kind of ambiguity which we meet in other churches of this period, an ambiguity arising from failure to reconcile aesthetic needs—in particular, a desire for bi-axial symmetry—with traditional orientation. It is true that Wren, in his report for the guidance of architects engaged on "Queen Anne's churches", had recommended that porticos should disregard internal arrangements and stand where they would be most effective, and Hawksmoor had followed this advice in St. George's, Bloomsbury. But the proof of the pudding is in the eating, and the ingredients of Horbury church were not, one feels, very well stirred. At the same time the interior, as even Whitaker recognized, is with its exquisite plasterwork of an elegance not often surpassed.

* * *

Several large town churches with unorthodox plans were built during the latter part of the eighteenth century. The octagonal form, which John Wesley thought the best of all for preaching, was followed in St. Mary's, Birmingham, (demolished in 1925). Designs for this church, one of a pair of chapels built to relieve the pressure on Birmingham's two parish churches, were solicited in 1772, "the said Chapel to be built in an Octagon or any other Form as the said Architects shall think proper, and to contain 1,000 sittings". As built, St. Mary's could hold a congregation of nearly 1,700. To judge from photographs, it was not very elegant; William Hutton thought that it was "in an airy situation and taste, but shows too little steeple and too much roof". The land on which the church stood was given by a certain Mary Weaman—hence, following a custom of compliment not uncommon in the eighteenth century, the dedication. Most of the funds for its erection were raised by subscription, subscribers of £20 or more becoming trustees for the building, but resort was had to more picturesque methods also, as is recorded in the *Birmingham Gazette* of Sept. 12, 1774:

> "On Wednesday last the Musical Entertainments began here, when Handel's Grand Dettingen Te Deum, Jubilate and Coronation Anthem, were performed in St. Philip's Church to a crowded and respectable Audience, and in the Evening at the New Theatre, Alexander's Feast was exhibited with great Applause.—On Thursday morning, at St. Philip's Church, the Oratorio of Judas Maccabaeus;

56 St. Paul, Liverpool, 1769, by Thomas Lightholler
Demolished 1932

57 Knutsford, Cheshire, 1744

58 Christchurch, Cambridge, Massachusetts, U.S.A., 1761

59 St. Martin, Worcester, 1768-72, by Anthony Keck

GIBBS'S INFLUENCE IN THE TREATMENT OF THE INTERIOR

and in the Evening, at the Theatre, a Grand Miscellaneous Concert, was performed to a very brilliant and numerous Company, with reiterated Plaudits, in which the Vocal Performers, particularly Miss Davis, and Mrs. Wrighten discovered very capital Powers; and the Instrumental Performance in general gave the highest satisfaction.—And on Friday morning the Sacred Oratorio of Messiah was performed at the Church.—The Produce of the different Entertainments is supposed to amount to about 800*l.*, which sum is to be applied towards the Completion of St. Mary's Chapel.—The Balls on Wednesday and Thursday Evenings were uncommonly splendid, and were honoured with the Presence of many Persons of the first Rank and Distinction in this Kingdom."

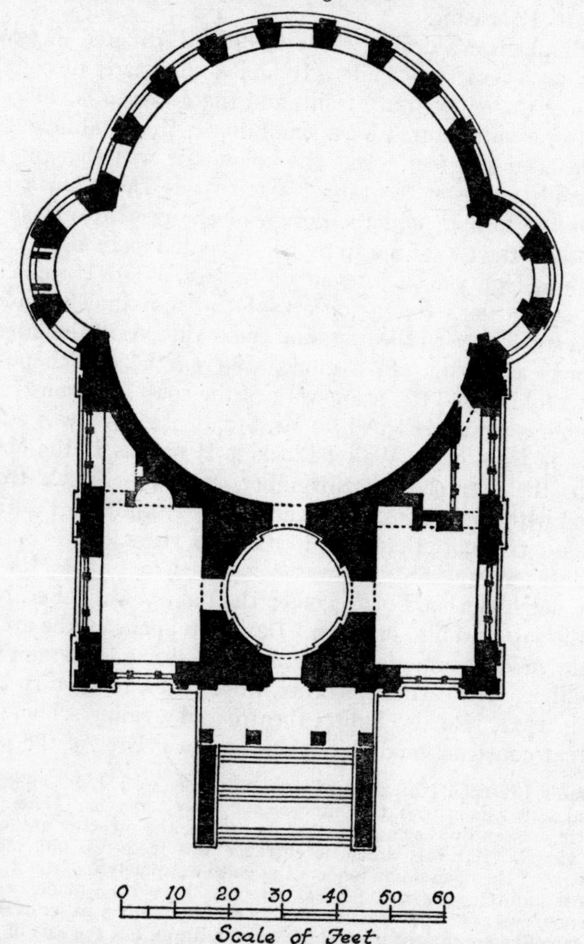

All Saints' church, Newcastle, 1786, designed by David Stephenson: plan
The altar stands in the apse to the right (Redrawn from T. Sopwith, *The church of All Saints' Newcastle*)

The elliptical church of All Saints', Newcastle-on-Tyne (60), unlike St. Mary's, Birmingham, represents the rebuilding of a parish church which had fallen into decay. A competition was held in 1786, when plans were submitted by five architects, Bell, Dobbs, Dopling, Harrison and Stephenson. The final choice lay between the designs of David Stephenson and Thomas Harrison. It seems that Harrison's would have been selected but for the expense of its execution; it was for a semicircular church, and we are told that "the chord line formed the south front, and was adorned with a handsome Doric portico". One could wish that the drawings still existed, for Thomas Harrison ("of Chester") is an interesting figure. Of humble birth, he had been sent to Rome by Lawrence Lord Dundas, where he had attracted the notice of Pope Clement XIV and been made a member of the Academy of St. Luke. In 1786 he was forty-two—he lived to be eighty-five—and was practising at Lancaster.

David Stephenson's design, as first adopted, differed in two respects from the church as it was built. It had a colonnade of coupled Ionic columns along the entire south front, and there was to have been a plain octagonal tower surmounted by a small dome, the total height of which would have been 143 feet. But the colonnade was thought to be too expensive and the tower too tame; a tetrastyle Doric portico was substituted for the former, and the design of the present steeple, which is 202 feet high to the top of the spire, was accepted in 1790. The elliptical nave measures eighty-six by seventy-two feet. The longer chord runs north and south along the major axis of the church as a whole, but the altar is in a small apse to the east, and the main axis of the interior of the nave is thus east-west. In a monograph on the church published in 1826 we are told that "the framework of the roof . . . constructed from a very ingenious model designed by Mr. Stephenson . . . was put together in the area, in front of Sir Walter Blackets Hospitals, in the Manors, and placed on the church, in November, 1787". Much trouble was experienced with the accoustics of the building, and the position of the pulpit was altered more than once in its early years.[1]

All Saints', Newcastle (60), was completed in 1796.[2] Its total cost was in the neighbourhood of £27,000; the money was raised by a parish rate and the sale and hire of pews. David Stephenson, the architect—he received the modest sum of £300 for the job—was a local man who began as a carpenter. His earliest recorded work was a temporary bridge over the Tyne in 1772. He also built a theatre and a riding school; evidently he had great constructional ability and was a master of the problems of

[1] In St. Paul's, Liverpool (56), a domed church designed by T. Lightholler, consecrated in 1769, and destroyed in 1932, the pulpit was actually movable. It had "a staircase in the centre, unseen by the congregation, by which, the preacher gradually ascends to public view". But this dramatic entrance was it seems, but the prelude to anticlimax, for "the open dome renders the voice extremely indistinct, and in some parts almost unintelligible". "Several attempts have been made to remedy this inconvenience," we are told, "particularly by spreading oiled paper over the bottom of the concave like parchment upon the head of a drum, but the ears of the audience are not so much benefitted, as their sight is offended by this contrivance."

[2] "1796, October 21—When the round stone on the top of All Saints' steeple was laid by the workmen, John Burdikin, a private in the Cheshire Militia, raised his body upon his head, resting upon that stone, and his feet in the air, where he remained for some time in that position and situation! He is now a hairdresser in Gateshead." (Oliver's *Newcastle Guide*).

60 All Saints, Newcastle, 1786-96, by David Stephenson
From an engraving by M. Lambert, after T. Sopwith

61 Banbury, Oxfordshire, 1790-7, by Samuel Pepys Cockerell:
the interior looking east, before the alterations of 1858-73
From an early nineteenth century engraving

62 St. Chad, Shrewsbury, 1790-2, by George Steuart

roofing large areas. John Dobson, the famous architect of early Victorian Newcastle, was his pupil.

The designer of St. Chad's, Shrewsbury (62), a church of similar size, is a somewhat obscure figure. His name was George Steuart, and he died in 1806 at Douglas, Isle of Man. His domestic work included the country houses of Attingham, Shropshire, and Earl Stoke, Wiltshire. He also designed the parish church of Wellington, Shropshire (1788), the interior of which is of the ordinary basilican form with lateral galleries supported by columns and in their turn supporting arcades; on plan the church is a T, having a short cross-piece containing the vestries and main entry, with the tower over, at the west end, and a feature of the exterior is the series of shallow arched recesses binding together the two ranges of windows.

St Chad's, Shrewsbury, an altogether more remarkable design, has a circular nave—a peculiarity which occasionally gets it a mention in the text-books. The practicability of this solution of the problem of accommodating a large congregation must have exercised the minds of many architects at this time; a London church in which it was applied was St. Peter-le-Poer, Broad Street (designed by Jesse Gibson in 1788; destroyed in 1908) where, however, the rotunda, hidden away behind the entrance façade, made no contribution to the external effect. St. Chad's, which was built in 1790-2, stands free of buildings on all sides, on a splendid site above the Severn. Steuart made the most of his opportunity, and his church is one of the most boldly conceived buildings of the whole Georgian epoch. While it possesses the usual attributes of "Adam" architecture, it combines with them, in the simplicity of its masses, the grand sweep of the nave cornice, and the weighty severity of the tower—so different from the picturesque steeple of All Saints', Newcastle—a monumentality which we may not always associate with the style. Inside, the elliptical vestibule, with twin staircases leading to the gallery, is a particularly successful feature.

The erection of St. Chad's was superintended by John Simpson, the engineer of the Caledonian Canal. This explains the fine quality of the masonry and of the general workmanship throughout. The "Robinsonian order"[1] of the columns supporting the nave ceiling is explained by their iron cores, although, as may be seen in the exterior of the church and elsewhere, Steuart favoured an attenuated order even when it was not necessary to avoid obstructing the view. The total cost was £17,752, which would not seem to have been excessive for so solidly built a church which could hold 1,750 people in the pews and 400 in free sittings.

So far we have examples of the octagon, the ellipse, and the circle. For a square church of comparable size we may go to Banbury (61). The nave of Banbury parish church was built in 1790-7 to the design of Samuel Pepys Cockerell; its tower was added by that architect's more famous son, Charles Robert Cockerell, in 1822.

The favourite laudatory epithets of later Georgian writers, "elegant", "chaste", "neat", are scarcely descriptive of Banbury church, and one

[1] Sir Thomas Robinson was a very tall man. Lord Chesterfield, passing Ripley's Admiralty one day, glanced up at the elongated columns of the portico and remarked that they were, he supposed, of the Robinsonian order.

suspects that its early admirers were compelled to fall back on "handsome". For Cockerell, true in this to his training by the conservative Sir Robert Taylor, made no concessions to the contemporary taste for elegance, chastity, and neatness. With its heavily rusticated, somewhat forbidding exterior—"more like a gaol than a Christian temple", thought a *Gentleman's Magazine* correspondent in 1800—Banbury church shows another characteristic of certain of the architecture of the time, a characteristic which probably derived from the fantasies of Piranesi—the exploitation of the drama of sheer size. The great scale is maintained within. The nave is ninety feet square internally, with twelve columns of the Composite order forming an inner square. The columns are so disposed that the arches connecting the eight innermost of them form on plan an equal-sided octagon, and in the octagon, over the central space of the nave, is a shallow dome. This scheme results in the middle bay on each side being wider than the rest ; these middle bays are barrel-vaulted, while the others are roofed with groined cross-vaults. The planning of the interior as a whole has the kind of logic which pertains to all central-domed churches. It differs from Wren's designs in the *genre* in its lack of directional emphasis. Until 1858 there was a fourth gallery, containing the organ, across the east end, and the communion table was tucked away underneath it ; the present chancel was added in 1873 by Sir Arthur Blomfield, who was also responsible for the polychromatic decorations. In his London churches—even those with central domes—Wren always contrived to stress the importance of the west-to-east axis, leading to the altar as a focal point. A hundred years later the new classicism could express itself without having to cater for a need which, it would seem, churchmen no longer felt with any acuteness.

* * *

These buildings, with their theatre-like naves, are the Anglican counterparts of such churches of Lutheran Germany as the square Garnisonkirche at Potsdam and the oval Pauluskirche at Frankfurt-on-Main. Most of the larger churches of the period were more conventional in plan, even if their internal arrangements, and in particular the prominence given to the pulpit—in St. Paul's, Leeds, for instance, it was on the east wall above the communion table—would strike most people today as odd. The cruciform type, which is not too suitable for a building intended mainly as a preaching-house and in Germany had been condemned by the influential writer Leonard Christoph Sturm, lingered on, sanctioned by long tradition. St. George's Reforne, Portland, is a cruciform church of 1777, with a central dome, an apse, and a western tower ; the builder's name was Gilbert.

But the aisled nave, with or without a structural chancel, remained the most common plan for churches of any pretensions to size. Kirkleatham (69), near Middlesbrough, has a handsome church of this type dating from 1763 ; it was designed by Robert Corney,[1] of whom nothing else seems to be known. (Anyone asked to guess its architect would probably name John Carr, and Carr did, as it happens, recast

[1] I am indebted to Mrs. Katharine A. Esdaile for this information.

63 Horbury, Yorkshire, 1791, by John Carr of York

64 Binley, Warwickshire, 1771-3, perhaps by Robert Adam

THE ADAMESQUE INTERIOR

65 Over Whitacre, Warwickshire, 1766

66 Tardebigge, Worcestershire, 1777,
by Francis Hiorn of Warwick

Kirkleatham Hall for Sir Thomas Turner, who rebuilt the church and part of the village, on " model " lines, at about the same time.)

The interior of Kirkleatham church follows the column and lintel system of construction. Alongside this system, internal arcades remained in use well on into George III's reign—as we shall see at St. Thomas's, Bristol. Nor was the compromise employed by Gibbs in St. Martin's-in-the-Fields and elsewhere, in which the vaulting springs from square blocks of entablature, soon abandoned. St. Martin's, Worcester, built 1768-72, has the device translated into the Ionic order (59), together with the rusticated windows of its metropolitan namesake. This is a church of red brick with stone dressings ; it has a plain west tower. Its designer was Anthony Keck, among whose recorded works were the Worcester County Infirmary and Dr. Thomas Nash's house, Beverey, an engraving of which appears on the title page of its owner's monumental *Worcestershire* (1781). He built another church, described as " very small", at Flaxley, in the Forest of Dean, but this made way for an edifice by Sir Gilbert Scott in 1856.

The Gibbs tradition died hard ; the nave of St. Paul's, Birmingham, built 1777-9 by Roger Eykyn, a Staffordshire man, might on the evidence of style be antedated forty years.[1] In the 'eighties it was carried on, and developed in a rather charming way, by Thomas Hardwick at Wanstead, Essex. In Thomas Hardwick (1752-1829) the two centuries and the two orthodoxies, Palladian and Greek, met, for he was a pupil of Sir William Chambers and the father of Philip Hardwick, designer of the Doric " arch " at Euston and of the other works of the London and Birmingham Railway. And it was Thomas Hardwick's office that J. M. W. Turner entered, intending to become an architect ; Hardwick advised him to be a painter. Wanstead church (73) is one of Hardwick's early works. It was begun in 1787 and finished in three years. The walls are of brick, faced with Portland stone ; at the west end is a Roman Doric porch and over the west gable a small Ionic cupola of wood and copper. The nave is of five bays, with a flat ceiling over the central part and groined vaults over the galleried aisles, and there is quite a spacious chancel. Of the fittings the pulpit, with its sounding board amusingly poised on two "palm tree " columns, is the most notable ; the former east window by Francis Eginton has gone the way of too much Georgian painted glass.

As a miniature St. Martin's-in-the-Fields of this time we may cite Badminton church, whose highly ornamental interior derives from Gibbs's design even to the point of having saucer-domes over the aisles (71). Badminton was built some four years before Wanstead, but it is convenient to depart from chronology here to group it with Christ Church, Bristol, because the same architect must surely have been responsible for both. The Bristol church is known to have been designed by William Paty in 1792. The Patys were a prominent family of sculptors and builders in eighteenth-century Bristol. William was the son of Thomas Paty, who was employed by the elder Wood on the Bristol Exchange as " ornament carver ", and who designed and built St. Michael's in the same city in an

[1] The really excellent steeple was added by Francis Goodwin in 1823.

odd blend of Gothic and Doric. Christ Church has an unusally massive-looking tower, of the full width of the church, surmounted by a high spire. The interior of the nave, which is smaller than this steeple would lead one to expect, is again closely based on St. Martin's-in-the-Fields, but the extreme elongation of the columns (emphasized to an unfortunate degree by the removal of the original high pews), together with the tenuity of the ornament and detail generally, shows that a radical change had overtaken English architecture since Gibbs's day.

Bristol is rich in eighteenth-century architecture, and not least in churches. Contemporary with Christ Church is St. Thomas's, which was opened in 1793. Its architect, James Allen, was described by *The New Bristol Guide* as " an ingenious, scientific, and the principal architect of Bristol".

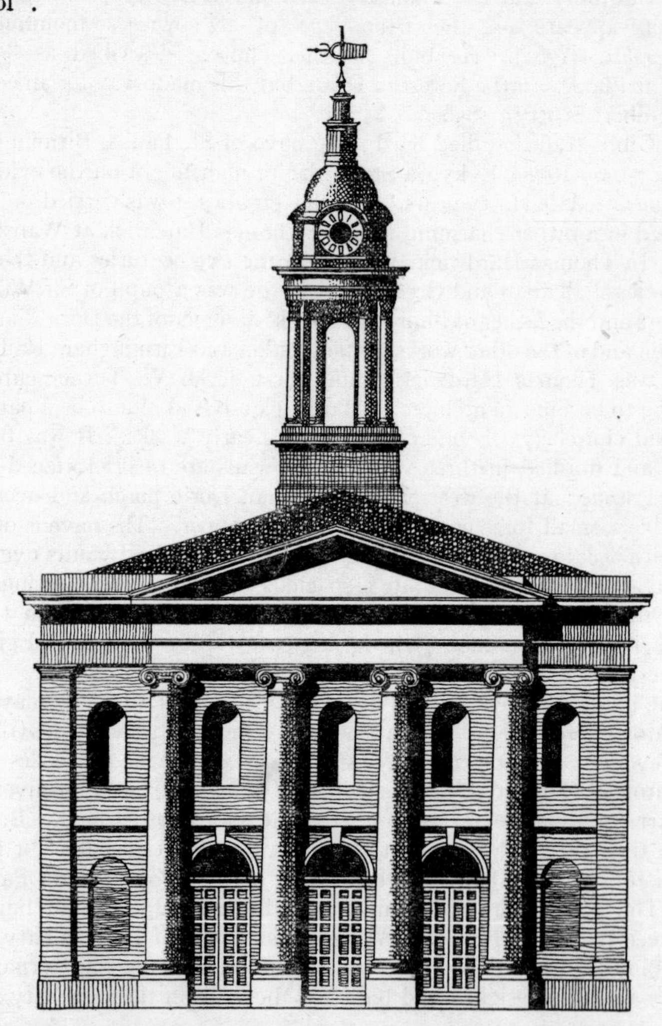

All Saints', Southampton, designed by Willey Reveley, 1792 : the west elevation
Destroyed by bombing, 1941 (Redrawn from C. L. Stieglitz, *Plans et Dessins*, 1800)

St. Thomas's is a larger church than Christ Church, and it retains its medieval tower. It comprises an aisled nave of five bays, and a chancel, The nave and the chancel are covered by a single barrel-vault, with transverse ribs springing from cornices which run the length of the church on either side; these cornices break forward at the springing of each rib above the pillars of the arcades, and there is a cherub's head under each break. The nave is lighted partly by windows in the vault—a system which was employed often enough by Wren and others in London but is not very common in the provinces, where the problem of obtaining sufficient light was not generally so acute. The aisles are much lower than the nave and have flat ceilings; externally, the different roof levels are linked by curved ramps. The only exterior elevation that is at all elaborated is the east end of the chancel, which faces the street; its lowest division is plain wall, the next is treated as a huge Venetian window, blind but for a circular opening in the head of the middle compartment, and above this is a festoon flanked by recessed panels.

But this kind of church, with its arcades and Roman vault, was soon to be outmoded. On the one hand, the influence of Greek architecture led to a general preference for colonnaded treatment, with flat or only slightly curved ceilings. On the other, increased science on the constructional side, coupled with the use of Baltic pine, made possible the abolition of internal supports altogether, even in the largest churches. The former tendency is illustrated by Thomas Telford's church at Bridgnorth, designed in 1798. Its very plain interior has Ionic colonnades, while the exterior, completely lacking in Adam "elegance", is solid and imposing in the way that Smirke's churches are solid and imposing; altogether it points forward unmistakably to the Commissoners' churches of twenty and more years later. Of the enlarged meeting-house type of church, galleried but without internal columns, All Saints', Southampton, begun in 1792 by Willey Reveley, was perhaps the finest example of this period. It was a casualty of the bombs, but its plan and elevations may still be studied in that curious Anglophil production of 1800, C. L. Stieglitz's *Plans et Dessins tirés de la Belle Architecture.* It had an engaged Ionic portico at the west end, a cupola at the east, and a segmental ceiling spanning sixty-one feet.

* * *

The famous Battle of the Styles, Classical *versus* Gothic, raged in the second quarter of the nineteenth century. The controversy which led to the ousting of Roman models by those of Greece was of a more academic nature and, although it had its violent phases, resembled a war of attrition rather than a battle. On the continent, nationalist sentiments increased the ardour with which the two sides urged their respective cases, because the French, led by Le Roy, whose *Les plus beaux Monuments de la Grèce* was published in 1758, were the self-appointed champions of Greece, while the Italians, with Piranesi conspicuous among them, defended the conception of Roman—and thus Italian—supremacy. In England the affair was rather involved. For Robert Adam, the friend of Piranesi, was on good terms with James Stuart, the author of the text of *The Antiquities of Athens* (which, appearing in 1762, superseded Le Roy's book as the standard work on Greek architecture), and " did him the doubtful honour of absorbing his cherished Greek *motifs* into a style which was fundamentally the very antithesis of Stuart's ideals".[1] But Sir William Chambers would have no truck with anything Greek. In the 1791 edition of his

Ayot St. Lawrence, Hertfordshire, 1778-9, designed by Nicholas Revett: the interior looking towards the apse, after a drawing by C. H. B. Quennell

Treatise on the Decorative Part of Civil Architecture there is a bitter attack on the *Gusto Greco*. Chambers states that he had intended to include it in the 1768 edition, but had suppressed it then because he believed that Greek architecture was already a lost cause; and there exists the draft of a lecture, composed by him about that date, in which he professed the view that " they might with equal success oppose a Hottentot and a Baboon to the Apollo and the Gladiator as set up the Grecian architecture against the Roman". " It hath afforded Occasion of Laughter to every

[1] Miss Lesley Lawrence, " Stuart and Revett," *Warburg Institute Journal*, 1938-9.

67 St. Chad, Shrewsbury, 1790-2, by George Steuart; the circular nave from the gallery

68 Brandsby-cum-Stearsby, Yorkshire, 1767, by Thomas Atkinson of York

Photo: F. Frith & C

69 Kirkleatham, Yorkshire, 1763, by Robert Corney (Mausoleum, 1740)

Two northern churches by local architects

intelligent Architect", wrote this splenetic opponent of eighteenth-century "modernismus", "to see with what Pomp the Grecian antiquities have lately been ushered into the World and what Encomiums have been lavished upon things that in Reality deserve little or no Notice".

When Chambers composed the lecture quoted, the *Gusto Greco* had scarcely affected church architecture. Indeed, there was perhaps only one church which showed any conspicuous Greek influence. In 1764 the Earl of Harcourt, engaged in the improvement of his park at Nuneham Courtenay, had demolished the old church of the place and proceeded to erect a classical building in its stead (78). It is said that the design was based on a suggestion by the earl himself; the architect was James Stuart.

Of Nuneham Courtenay, Horace Walpole, in 1780, wrote enthusiastically: "The place is more Elysian than ever, the river full to the brim, and the church by one touch of Albano's pencil, is become a temple, and a principal feature of one of the most beautiful landscapes in the world." As the quotation suggests, what the Earl wanted most from his new church was a portico that should be a "principal feature" in the masterpiece of landscape gardening which Capability Brown had created for him. And this being so, it is beside the point to complain that the portico shelters nothing but a blank wall and constitutes a quite gratuitous addition to the design of the church as a whole (if not indeed a somewhat confusing one). However, interest does not stop at the portico—perhaps the earliest hexastyle Greek Ionic portico in England and extremely graceful—or at the semi-circular porch to the west. At first sight the church that lies behind them looks rather like a Byzantine church clothed in Greek mouldings and worked out with a Greek precision, so that—since Stuart could hardly have avoided noticing the many Byzantine churches of Athens—one might imagine that it represented a synthesis of the traveller's visual impressions. However, to enter it is to discover that the dome rises, not over a square in the Byzantine manner, but from a rotunda in the Roman. If this little building's grandest relative on the maternal side is the Erechtheum, on the paternal it is the Pantheon, not Sancta Sophia.

The church at Ayot St. Lawrence (102), which was designed by Nicholas Revett, Stuart's collaborator in *The Antiquities of Athens*, came into being in much the same way as the one at Nuneham Courtenay. For it was built, in 1778-9, at the expense of Sir Lionel Lyde, who thought that the old village church was more ornamental in ruins. It is the latest of Revett's known executed designs, although he did not die until thirty years after its completion. The detail of the exterior is of course impeccably Greek, the order of the Doric portico being that of the Temple of Apollo at Delos. (The columns of this order, which Revett employed elsewhere, have narrow bands of fluting at the top and bottom, a peculiarity presumably due to their having never been finished). But the open screens connecting the body of the church with the tombs on either side would have been thought a strange feature by any citizen of ancient Delos. Miss Lesley Lawrence has remarked of these screens that they seem "to recall the bare ruins of colonnades as Revett must so often have seen them" during his sojourn in Greece; this reproduction of fortuitous effects in the new church is related to their preservation in the old as the

Ayot St. Lawrence, Hertfordshire, 1778-9, designed by Nicholas Revett: entrance front, after a drawing by C. H. B. Quennell

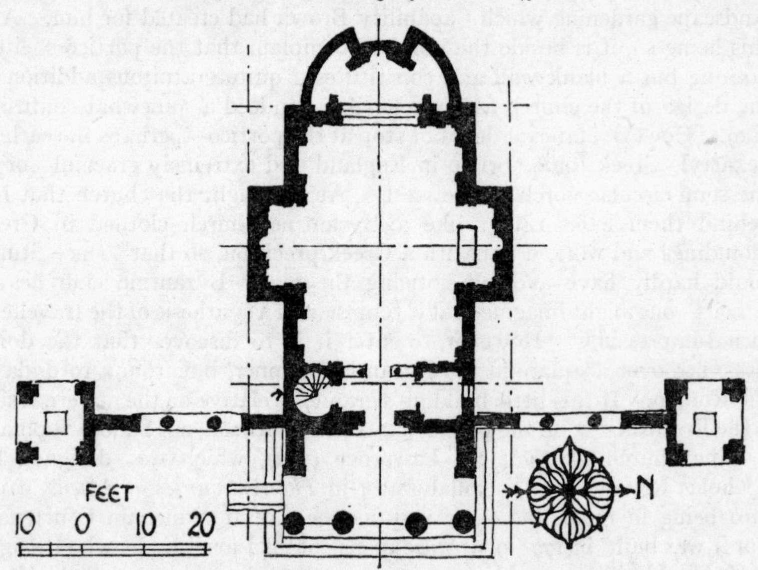

Ayot St. Lawrence, Hertfordshire, 1778-9, designed by Nicholas Revett: plan after C. H. B. Quennell

obverse and reverse of the contemporary romantic spirit. Revett's building is, in fact, the familiar Palladian scheme of *corps de logis* and supporting pavilions translated into terms of a small church, dressed up in Greek detail, and set down in an English park to terminate the view—a function which it performs exquisitely. Unlike any Greek building that ever was, it was designed to be seen from one quarter of the compass only—the entablature stops short half-way along each side of the nave—while the interior, with its arched recesses and ingenious apse with advanced back wall, could only belong to an age familiar with the planning of the Roman *thermae*.

70 St. Lawrence, West Wycombe, Buckinghamshire, opened 1763

71 Badminton, Gloucestershire, 1763

72 Hardenhuish, Wiltshire, 1779,
by John Wood the younger of Bath

73 Wanstead, Essex, 1787-90, by Thomas Hardwick

The unfluted and comparatively slender columns of the Temple of Apollo at Delos, dating from the fourth century before Christ, were doubtless more readily acceptable to eyes accustomed to Roman proportions than the more massive Doric of the fifth century. The first English church in which the latter appears would seem to be that at Great Packington, Warwickshire (76, 80), built in 1790 by the Earl of Aylesford to the design of Joseph Bonomi, an Italian who in 1767 had accepted an invitation to join the Adam brothers and, after working with them for several years, had set up in practice on his own account. This too, is a park church, and it is remote from the nearest village. Built in red brick with sandstone dressings, it is planned as a square containing an equal-armed cross, with four pediments and four squat, lead-domed towers. At each corner of the central part of the nave, which is solidly vaulted in brick faced with stone—no structural timber is used in the building—stands a fluted Doric column carrying a portion of entablature.

The Greek Revival was so slow in getting under way that Greek Doric columns still seemed a daring novelty when Sir John Soane used them in the Bank of England fourteen years after Packington church was built. Soane never reached Greece on his travels, and his favourite version of the Doric order was that of the Temple of Poseidon at Paestum. We find him employing it in the church that he designed for Tyringham about 1796. Unfortunately this design was never executed, because it was found cheaper to repair the old church, and so we have been denied the one ecclesiastical building in which this great architect would not have had to comply with the bleakly utilitarian requirements of the 1818 Church Building Act.

Arthur Bolton showed that the germ of the idea of Soane's Tyringham design, with its central dome and three porches, is to be found in a French work of 1753, the Abbé Laugier's *Essai sur L'Architecture*. Soane himself termed it a "sepulchral church", and in so doing he may well have had in mind engravings after the drawings of another Frenchman, Jacques François Blondel, whose fancy revelled in vast, dramatically lit interiors of buildings of this description. But J. M. Gandy's interior view of the proposed Tyringham church (104), with its lounging ladies and prim Georgian parson and clerk, has, it must be confessed, little in common with the heroic imaginings of the French architect.

* * *

The "sepulchral church" scheme was naturally attractive to the rich landowner, who saw in it a means of simultaneously demonstrating his piety, perpetuating his taste, and commemorating his name. Another example of the type is the church of Strathfieldsaye, Hampshire, which was built in 1784 at the expense of Thomas Pitt, later Lord Camelford, to a cruciform plan with a shallow central dome resting on an octagonal drum. Perhaps Pitt was his own architect. At Stowe he designed the Corinthian arch which stands at the end of the Buckingham avenue, and he collaborated in the design of the south front of the house itself. Incidentally, it was largely owing to him that Soane was appointed architect to the Bank of England.)

At West Wycombe, Buckinghamshire, there is a church (70, 85) which in many respects is as unorthodox as were the pursuits of Sir Francis Dashwood, of Hell Fire Club notoriety, at whose expense it was built. Externally, its oddest feature is the hollow ball of gilt wood that crowns the tower. The plan was to some extent dictated by the outline of the old church on the site, part of the tower and the chancel of which were incorporated in the new. The nave is a spacious hall of sixty by forty feet surrounded by sixteen Corinthian columns, which support an elaborately enriched entablature, and covered by a ceiling painted to imitate coffering, while the walls are adorned with plaster swags of fruit and flowers; in the chancel, which is entered through a low and narrow arch, the chief ornament is a ceiling panel of the Last Supper. This church, like that of Mereworth, was never pewed; the contemporary account of its opening in 1763 tells us that there were "seats covered with green cloth, and hassocks to kneel on". Who designed it is a matter for conjecture.

Of the simpler kind of country church built in George III's reign some have made way for more pretentious though not more seemly edifices. Such was the fate of the diminutive version of St. Paul's, Covent Garden, contrived for Alderman Beckford at Fonthill Gifford, and of the tiny cruciform church built at Long Ditton, to the design of Sir Robert Taylor, in 1776. However, many survive. And of these one of the pleasantest is surely that at Chiselhampton, Oxfordshire, which dates from 1763. (74, 75). The cupola and delicately scrolled pediment at the west end of this little building have something of the unforced gaiety and grace which characterizes the contemporaneous colonial architecture of the New World, and as a whole it possesses for us today such obvious charm that it is hard to understand how a writer of half-a-century ago could dismiss it as "a modern church with a bell-turret such as is usually placed on stables".

Had the author of Murray's *Guide to Oxfordshire* been writing sixty years earlier his opinion would have been different, and his tone might have resembled that in which T. W. Horsfield in his *History of Sussex* describes Glynde: "The first object that attracts attention is the little church, built in 1765, at the expense of Dr. Trevor, then Bishop of Durham. The entrance, which is to the west, is formed by a neat portico, over which, sculptured in stone, are the Trevor arms, impaled by those of the See of Durham. The same coat is also exhibited in the windows. The interior is exquisitely neat, and strictly correspondent with the outward appearance of the edifice. Of the chancel window, composed of painted glass, decorated with sacred subjects, it is impossible to speak in terms too unmeasured. Every part of the edifice is alike distinguished by an elegant simplicity, which affords a striking contrast to the barbaric gloom which characterizes the great majority of Sussex churches".

Glynde church was designed by Lord Chesterfield's friend, Sir Thomas Robinson, whose best known work in architecture is the west gallery at Castle Howard—although his masterpiece may well have been the rotunda at Claydon House, which was demolished within a few years of its erection. The builders were John Morris and William Langridge, of Lewes, and the east window, which Horsfield admired so hugely, was by

74 Interior, looking west

75 Exterior, from the south-east

Chiselhampton, Oxfordshire, 1763

76 Great Packington, Warwickshire, 1790, by Joseph Bonomi

77 Avington, Hampshire. An unspoilt interior of 1779

78 All Saints, Nuneham Courtenay, Oxfordshire, 1764, by the first Earl of Harcourt, revised by James (" Athenian ") Stuart

79 Great Houghton, Northamptonshire, 1754 From an eighteenth century drawing
The urns on the tower have since been removed and
the nave has been "restored" in Norman style

80 Great Packington, Warwickshire, 1790, by Joseph Bonomi

William Peckitt. Ten years later Sir Thomas Robinson practically duplicated the Glynde design at his former seat of Rokeby in Yorkshire, in a little church which, sad to relate, underwent a stiff course of "amelioration" at the hands of the nineteenth century.

The cupola at Chiselhampton, and the simple bell-cotes at Glynde and Rokeby, are over the gable at the entrance end of the church, and this was the common arrangement. A more monumental effect was essayed at Brandsby, Yorkshire, where an octagonal cupola with a Doric order and an ogee dome surmounts a low square tower rising from the centre of the roof (68). Inside, the tower is supported by four Doric columns which form a square in the centre of the nave and are linked to each other and the lateral walls by groined vaults. The designer of Brandsby church, which dates from 1767, was Thomas Atkinson, a local architect who was engaged in Gothic works at Bishopthorpe, the Archbishop of York's palace, at about the same time.

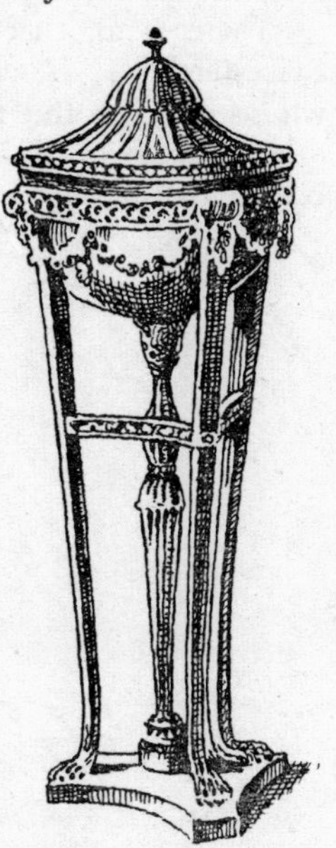

Font at Rokeby, 1775, designed by Sir Thomas Robinson After a drawing by J. C. Buckler

Other equally unpretentious churches were given substantial western towers. Generally these were plain affairs, with some kind of parapet and possibly urns at the corners, such as had been built ever since the Restoration. There is little enough about the battlemented tower of Avington, Hampshire (77), (a church chiefly remarkable for retaining all its original furnishings) that would help one to assign it to its correct date—actually 1779. But the tower of the exactly contemporary church at Hardenhuish, Wiltshire (72), carries an octagonal cupola. The architect here was the younger John Wood of Bath; the purist might cavil at the Venetian windows in the lateral walls, but Wood evidently felt that a free combination of Palladian features was all that was called for in a building of this size. In his earlier church at Woolley, built in 1761, he combined, even more waywardly, classical cupola and Gothic windows and arches (84).

A number of country churches had spires. The building of spires of one sort or another went on right through the classical period. Perhaps nothing shows more clearly the Englishman's tendency to regard buildings as incidents in the landscape, of which he has always had so real an appreciation. As a rule, the spires of the latter part of the eighteenth century are more frankly medieval in outline than those of the preceding age; their designers did not feel that it was incumbent on them to disguise them as classical obelisks. One of the most graceful steeples of the time belongs to Tardebigge, Worcestershire (66). The architect was Francis Hiorn, son of one of the builders of Daventry Church, and it dates from 1777. Did the same Hiorn also design the church at Over Whitacre, Warwickshire (65), which is eleven years older? At all events, the steeples of Over Whitacre and Tardebigge afford an interesting comparison—the earlier with its Gibbsian window architraves, spherical ornaments on the angles of the belfry, and general squareness; the later with its more strictly classical urns, slight Adam-style mouldings, and ingenious complexity of form.

There is another small classical church with a spire at Saxby, Leicestershire. It was built in 1788 and it is one of three churches for whose erection the fourth Earl of Harborough was responsible. The other two are of slightly earlier date. But they are both Gothic, and so belong to the next chapter.

81 Interior

:2

:xterior from
he south-west

roome d'Abitot
Vorcestershire
onsecrated 1763

83 Stapleford, Leicestershire, 1783, by George Richardson

84 Woolley, Bath, 1761, by John Wood the younger

Chapter V

THE GOTHIC REVIVAL

THIS is not the place to examine the origins and the wider aspects of the Gothic Revival, or to canvass the question whether the name by which we all know that peculiarly English manifestation of the romantic spirit is as truly descriptive as it is convenient. All that has been done elsewhere. It may be taken as agreed that the movement was for many years as much a part of literary as of architectural history, that antiquaries like à Wood,

Gothic screen designed by William Kent and erected in Gloucester Cathedral 1742
Removed early in the nineteenth century
(From Vardy's *Designs of Inigo Jones*)

Hearne, and Stukeley admired medieval architecture when most people of taste did not, and that since the year 1170 hardly a decade has passed without the erection of buildings which can only be called Gothic. Everyone knows, too, that in its early stages the Gothic Revival was not mainly concerned with church building, and can recognize in the curious object noted by Dr. Richard Pococke at Wroxton in 1756, a "Gothic open rotundo of Mr. Miller's design, in which he has practis'd curtains that by turning screws let down so as to afford shelter which ever way you please", a more typical product of those days than the Gothic tower which the same Mr. Miller added to the parish church there.

Yet during the eighteenth century a by no means negligible number of churches were built "in the modern Gothic order", as it was sometimes described by an age for whom an architecture without "orders" was unthinkable. Perhaps one might distinguish between those, on the one hand, which were built by rich landowners bent on "improvements" in the special sense, and on the other, those which were built by parish vestries simply to replace dilapidated medieval fabrics. The former, it might be argued, were Gothic because Gothic was new; the latter because Gothic was old. But I do not think that the distinction could be maintained. It is possible that more people than we realize, among the *cognoscenti* as well as the unlearned, shared the sentiments expressed by James Cawthorn, the master of Tonbridge School, in his poem *Of Taste*:

> "One might expect a sanctity of style
> August and manly in an holy pile,
> And think an architect extremely odd,
> To build a playhouse for the church of God;
> Yet half our churches, such the mode that reigns,
> Are Roman theatres, or Grecian fanes;
> Where broad-arch'd windows to the eye convey
> The keen diffusion of too strong a day;
> Where, in the luxury of wanton pride,
> Corinthian columns languish side by side,
> Clos'd by an altar exquisitely fine,
> Loose and lascivious as a Cyprian shrine."

That eighteenth-century Gothic appears to us not "august and manly", but essentially feminine, does not alter the case.

Sir William Wilson's church of St. Mary, Warwick, which has been discussed in an earlier chapter, was begun in 1694. The tower of St. Dunstan-in-the-East dates from 1698; St. Mary Aldermary, from 1711; and the tower of St. Michael, Cornhill, from 1721. The west towers of Westminster Abbey were designed in 1735. And to this list might be added a number of secular buildings from the first three decades of the century. But all these can really be seen only as isolated phenomena in the history of their time. If we must have a date for the "beginning" of the Gothic Revival, it would probably be best to put it somewhere in the seventeen-forties. Even then we should remember that it was not at this time a "movement" with all that the term generally implies; the early Revivalists had no sense of mission, no desire that Gothic should *supersede* the classical, or "regular", architecture in which most of them were so much more at home. That did not come until Pugin's day, nearly a hundred years later. But the seventeen-forties, with the publication of Batty Langley's *Gothic Architecture improved by Rules and Proportions* near their beginning and Horace Walpole's first Strawberry Hill alterations at their end, saw the execution of many more would-be Gothic designs than any previous decade of the century. And thereafter the stream was slowly but surely to grow.

* * *

85 The centre of the painted ceiling of the nave, West Wycombe, 1763

86 The fan-vaulted plaster ceiling of the nave, Hartwell, Buckinghamshire, 1753-6

87 Eccleston, Cheshire, 1809-13, by William Porden Demolished 1899
From a print after J. C. Buckler

88 Galby, Leicestershire, 1741, by the elder Wing of Leicester

Galby church, Leicestershire (88), dates from 1741. It was designed, according to John Throsby, the antiquary and topographer, by an architect of the name of Wing, and it was built at the expense of William Fortrey, the chief local landowner. What is known of the pursuits of the latter gentleman, who thirty years later was to erect another, more impressive church less than a mile away, puts it beyond doubt that Galby church was intended to be Gothic throughout. And from a distance, seen in outline, it might indeed be mistaken for a medieval building. On a nearer approach, however, it will be found that while the tracery of the nave windows is quite passable Perpendicular, the openings in the tower are of classical form and its pinnacles, which from afar are such telling features in the creation of a general Gothic effect, are elaborated with detail which can only be described as Chinese. Mixture of Gothic and Chinese detail was not unusual in secular buildings. But it is odd that it should occur in a church.

The chancel at Galby is genuinely medieval, because the incumbent at the time of the rebuilding proved intractable concerning some point at issue which has not come down. Mr. Fortrey, it seems, was of a retiring nature and rather easily put out. The story goes that he intended to rebuild yet another church at Billesdon, where also he owned property, but that he gave up this scheme on account of the rudeness of an inhabitant who accused him of trespassing while he was prospecting for a site.[1] His great interest was campanology; we are told that he was "possessed of all the anecdotes that remain" concerning Hugh Watts, founder of the original bells of St Margaret's, Leicester, and that he was the "patron and director" of Thomas Eayre, the founder of two additional bells for the same church, "the charge of which, and a great part of that of new-hanging the whole peal" were borne by him. In Galby church he hung six bells, in that at Norton—of which later—no less than ten. This gentle soul, as one imagines him to have been, died pathetically in 1783, from the results of a night's exposure following a fall down a flight of steps in his own garden when there was no-one about to help.

The next personality to be encountered—the early history of the Gothic Revival is inevitably to some extent an account of personalities—is rather different. Sanderson Miller, as we see him reflected in the letters of his friends,[2] was very much the man of the world. Born in 1717, he inherited his father's estate of Radway, Warwickshire, at the age of twenty, and was granted another forty-three years in which to enjoy life as a country gentleman could and to employ his talent for architectural design. His most ambitious work in the latter sphere was Hagley Hall for Lord Lyttelton. This, built in 1754-60, is a large Palladian mansion, of a type common at the time, with four corner towers. His County Hall at Warwick is also classical; the builders here were the brothers Hiorn. But it was as a Gothic expert that Miller, having demonstrated what he

[1] Thus Throsby, *Select Views in Leicestershire*, 1790. J. Nichols, however, *County of Leicester*, 1795-1815, says that he merely intended to augment the number of bells.

[2] L. Dickens and M. Stanton, *An Eighteenth-century Correspondence*, 1910.

meant by Gothic in his own house and in his tower at Edgehill, was most in demand among his large acquaintance. For John Ivory Talbot he remodelled the great hall at Lacock Abbey; for Lord Hardwicke he built a ruined castle at Wimpole; for Lord North at Wroxton he designed, besides the "rotundo" and the church tower already mentioned, a window for the reception of a collection of ancient glass in his Lordship's private chapel.

There is some irony in the fact that of all Sanderson Miller's authenticated ecclesiastical designs the tower of Wroxton church alone should survive in recognizable form. For his original tower, erected in the spring of 1747, fell down in the course of its first winter and had to be rebuilt. Miller's friends hastened to assure him that his reputation as an architect had not been hurt in its collapse. "The downfall of Wroxton Tower, my dear Miller," wrote Lord Deerhurst, "would have drawn an earlier Condolence from me had I come to the Knowledge of it sooner than I did. I am glad, indeed, that it was delayed so long as I can now assure you that your fame for Architecture is not at all diminished by it. A friend of mine, apprized of this accident came to me yesterday and told me that he was going to build a Gothic Front to a stable, and, that as no one was so great a Master of that Style as yourself, desired I would procure a draught of one from you."

Walpole, who disliked Miller, thought that his Wroxton tower was in "a good plain Gothic style", and it would be hard to find much more to say about it, either for or against. Between 1753 and 1756 Miller was employed by Lyttelton to embellish the church at Hagley. His work here was destroyed by Street in 1858. Dr. Pococke described it with enthusiasm: "The chancel is entirely new; the windows are adorn'd on the sides and every part with Gothic ornaments in hewn stone, and all the other parts of it is in stuco. On the ceiling and at each end are the arms of the paternal ancestors of the Lytteltons . . . . The east window is entirely of rich painted glass . . . . the whole border'd with blue, purple, and green glass, lately made at Stourbridge. The three windows on each side are in Gothic style, adorn'd likewise with bordering of colour'd glass thrown into pretty Gothic figures. The windows in the church are of the same style but plain, and the seats are in the Gothic taste. The gallery is very beautifully adorn'd with roses, ec., carved in the wood, and the Communion rail is of Gothic design."

Dr. Richard Pococke, Bishop of Ossory, while making his 1756 tour had reason to examine Miller's work with some attention, because Miller had "been so kind as to undertake" to design some alterations which he planned in Kilkenny cathedral. On September 29th, he visited Miller at Radway, and on the way there he saw at Kineton "a new Gothic church, built to a good old tower by the care of the worthy minister, Mr. Talbot, nephew to the late Lord Chancellor, with the help of some subscriptions, but chiefly . . . . at his own expence, on a very small living, not so good as a curacy". The design for this church too was by Miller. But the nineteenth century was not amused, and Kineton church today bears no resemblance to the building which Miller left, and whose exterior may still be seen in an old photograph hanging in the vestry—a modest affair in a very plain Gothic style, with a shallow transept but neither buttresses nor parapet.

Another new Gothic church seen by Pococke still remains practically as it was when he saw it. It is at Shobdon, Herefordshire (1, 89), and it was built by John, second Viscount Bateman, in 1753. Who designed it is a mystery which will possibly never be solved. Perhaps Miller did. Like Kineton church, it has a shallow transept. (The southern projection formed the Bateman family pew, and the northern a pew for the servants; both are entered by doors from the garden of Shobdon Court.) And the fact that Pococke does not name Miller as the architect proves nothing; neither does he mention him in connection with Kineton. But Richard Bentley, the dilettante son of the great scholar and one of the members of the Strawberry Hill "Committee of Taste", is as likely a candidate as any. Lord Bateman was a nephew of Walpole's friend, the Hon. Richard, or "Dickey" Bateman, whom Walpole "converted from a Chinese to a Goth," and for whom Bentley had designed a "cloister" at Windsor. Since he was also, as we learn from Walpole, "a favourite relation" of Dickey Bateman, what more likely than that the latter should have introduced Bentley to him when he decided to rebuild Shobdon church?

Whoever its architect, Shobdon church is a fascinating example of "rococo Gothic", and one of the most important survivals of its kind. The church that, with the exception of the tower, Lord Bateman pulled down to make way for it, possessed a Norman chancel arch and two doorways with elaborate carvings of the Kilpeck type; these were set up as a "terminary" in the park. Dr Pococke thought that the Norman tympana were "in a very bad taste", but for the new church he had nothing but praise. It was "in the Gothic style, and . . . . very finely finished within all in the same style, every part being embellished with Gothic ornaments; the east window . . . . all painted glass in very elegant taste, and the other windows . . . . ornamented with colour'd glass". And so for the most part it remains today, although a west gallery, in much the same style as the rest of the church, was added in 1810, and the painted glass in the east window has been changed.

For all its quatrefoils, cusps, and crockets, the interior of Shobdon church is much more Rococo than Gothic—a consideration which rather adds to the likelihood of Bentley having been its designer. The exactly contemporary church at Hartwell, Buckinghamshire, as befits its greater scale (99), represents an effort in the direction of more serious use of Gothic forms. Not that the Rococo element is absent—far from it. But there is nothing at Hartwell so shockingly "un-structural" as the triple arches which divide Shobdon nave from the chancel and transept.[1] The plan too (it was alleged) was taken from the chapter house at York.

Hartwell church was built, 1753-6, by Sir Henry Lee, various other members of the Lee family subscribing. The architect was Henry Keene, whose best-known works, such as High Wycombe Guildhall and the Observatory at Oxford, are classical. In 1752 Keene had been appointed

[1] It is worth noting that Bentley designed bookcases with *double* arches for Strawberry Hill. (See *The Architectural Review*, December 1945, p. 153).

Surveyor to the Dean and Chapter of Westminster Abbey. If at Hartwell he really was inspired by the York chapter house, he certainly took great liberties with his model, adding two towers—the eastern one contains the chancel and the western the main entry—inventing his own detail, and roofing the interior with elaborate fan vaulting of plaster. But literal copying was generally far from the intentions of any architect of this period who happened to be working in Gothic, and even when it was attempted, as in certain features at Strawberry Hill, in the absence of measured drawings the originals were of necessity often seen through the eyes of some topographical draughtsman or engraver who was not likely to be sensitive to the finer points of medieval design. Nobody could mistake Hartwell church for a medieval building of any sort. This is not only because the detail is "incorrect". The root of the matter lies rather in the fact that Keene was incapable of organizing the components of his design in any but a fundamentally classical manner. Hence the static quality of the exterior of Hartwell church, with the horizontal emphasis of its string courses and the corbel table which resembles a classical cornice as closely as it dares, the pinnacles which seem to hesitate about the propriety of breaking the skyline, and the appearance of exact calculation with which the windows take up their station in the walls. Hence too, in fulfilment of a classical urge towards bi-axial symmetry, the twin towers. Like most of the Gothic buildings of the eighteenth century, Hartwell church can be described as a classical design in fancy dress. But in doing so we should remember that its contemporaries may have regarded it rather differently—as a Gothic design disciplined by the rules which, they believed, all true art should obey. When Langley called his celebrated book "Gothic Architecture, *improved* by Rules and Proportions", he meant what he said. Gothic seemed to Langley, and to others like him nurtured in the classical tradition, a primitive and licentious style which was nevertheless capable of refinement and systematization on classical lines.[1]

The interior of Hartwell church is undeniably impressive and might well have been deemed to possess the "sanctity of style" that Cawthorn missed in classical churches of the time. Its most special feature, the plaster fan vaulting, belongs to a category which was better represented in private houses than in churches. But there is another example, equal in elaboration if not in size, over the chancel at Wicken, Northamptonshire.

Wicken church, as a tablet within it records, was "designed and built by Thomas Prowse Esqr., in the Year 1758 and finished after his Death" (which occurred in 1767). It has since been thoroughly "restored" and contains no fittings of interest. It consists of an aisled nave of three bays, a deep chancel, and a western tower. The nave is covered by a slightly pointed barrel vault of plaster, quite plain but for the rosettes from which candelabra formerly hung, and over the aisles are groined cross-vaults without ribs or any ornament at all; the vaulting springs from piers of four clustered shafts each, on high octagonal plinths, and from corbels on the aisle walls. The chancel, as mentioned, has a plaster fan vault.

[1] Lord Burlington, expressing admiration of the west front of Lincoln cathedral, said that its architect must have been conversant with the best Roman models.

89 Shobdon, Herefordshire, 1753 : the interior looking east

90 Stone, Staffordshire, 1754, by William Baker

91 Norton-by-Galby, Leicestershire, 1770, by Wing of Leicester

As a whole, Wicken church has less character than either Shobdon or Hartwell, and the Rococo element is quite absent. But its designer, Thomas Prowse of Wicken Park, is of some interest as another of those amateurs who played so prominent a part in the earliest stage of the Gothic Revival. He possibly designed the little classical church at Berkley, Somerset (54), for which county he was several times Member of Parliament, and he was a close friend of Sanderson Miller, to whom he gave advice concerning the designs of Hagley and of Warwick County Hall. He was evidently acquainted with his neighbour antiquary, the formidable Browne Willis (who himself built a small church at Fenny Stratford, now incorporated as an aisle in the nineteenth-century building) and presumably with Walpole's correspondent the Rev. William Cole, who mentions his death in his *Blecheley Diary*.

With the church at Croome D'Abitot, Worcestershire (81, 82), built at the expense of the Earl of Coventry in 1761-3, we return from the amateur to the professional. Or so it would seem at first sight, since the most tangible existing evidence bearing on the question of the authorship of the design, in the shape of some drawings in Sir John Soane's Museum, seems to point to Robert Adam as architect. But Arthur Bolton showed that the plan attached to the faculty to take down and rebuild Croome church, which was granted in 1758, was for a classical building, considerably smaller than the Gothic one erected.[1] And among Coventry's intimate friends was Sanderson Miller, who may have been responsible for the general design of Croome Court (although the authorship of that too is a vexed question), so that it is a likely hypothesis that it was Miller who " converted him to a Goth " in the matter of the church, which may thus be the outcome of some sort of collaboration between Miller and Adam. Anyhow, it is a delightful building. The exterior, or at least the tower (81), is a relatively convincing essay in medievalism, showing in its pierced parapet and belfry window tracery what might be a reminiscence of fifteenth-century Somerset work ; pictorially it is much assisted by being exquisitely placed on a rise of the ground in the Capability Brown park. Inside there is nothing that anyone could ever have supposed medieval for an instant. The clustered columns in the nave support longitudinal lintels which are simply classical entablatures enriched with friezes of intersecting arches ; the ceilings are of elliptical section, and the delicately modelled plaster crockets round chancel arch and windows are Gothic in allusion rather than by imitation (82).

* * *

There is little structural boldness in any of these churches. But the second church to be built at the expense of William Fortrey, at King's Norton, Leicestershire, had a measure of it—indeed, rather too much, since the spire which formerly rose from its tall and slender tower had to be taken down for safety's sake. (For the same reason the number of bells had to be reduced from ten to eight). The architect was Wing of Leicester, who was the son of the Wing who rebuilt Galby church for Fortrey, and the date of the building about 1770.

[1] *The Architecture of Robert and James Adam*, 1922.

Though deprived of its spire, King's Norton church still remains in other respects exactly as Wing left it (91, 92, 93). It is rather different from any other early Gothic Revival church we have yet noticed. In plan it is a plain rectangle without structural chancel or aisles, with a narrower tower at the west end. There is nothing remarkable in that. But some of the detail of the exterior suggests that Wing, or perhaps Mr. Fortrey, had a more observant eye for Gothic than was usual at that time. The great size of the windows, too, is something new—the east end is nearly all window, with an ambitious effort in geometrical tracery in the centre—and, together with the stepped buttresses and pinnacles, is indicative of the fascination exercised throughout the early phases of the Revival by late Perpendicular buildings such as St. George's Chapel, Windsor, and the chapel of King's College, Cambridge. The church stands rather high, the appearance of precariousness which it shares with all eighteenth-century Gothic churches being thereby emphasized. (With its spire it must have looked even more precarious than in fact it was). The approach to the only entrance, which is in the base of the tower, lies between gate-piers which are topped by pineapples and on which hang a fine pair of wrought-iron gates, brought by Mr. Fortrey from Norton Old Hall, and up a balustraded flight of steps. To enter the church is to find oneself in another age; let John Throsby speak for it: "The inside, which has only one fine spacious aisle, is in the true quakerly neatness; the pews of oak; the pulpit is in the middle, corresponding with the neat altar-piece. It is, upon the whole, one of the compleatest churches in Leicestershire, of its size, I have seen". Nothing has been changed, neither the pews, nor the central three-decker, nor the Doric gallery, nor the altar rails and chancel gates, which alone of all the woodwork depart from the classicism of which the balustrades to the outside steps and the churchyard gates and gate-piers are an extension into the open air. The little would-be Perpendicular font survives in its original position under the gallery. And there is no Victorian glass.

The central pulpit, as still to be seen at King's Norton, was common in the eighteenth century. In the two Gothic churches erected by the fourth Earl of Harborough during the following decade, one in Leicestershire and one just over the Rutland border, less usual arrangements obtain.

The Rev. Robert Sherard succeeded to the Earldom of Harborough and its Leicestershire estates in 1770, but it was not until a dozen years later that he entered on his programme of church building, or rather re-building. This was, as we have seen, to include a classical structure for the parish of Saxby. But the first church to which he turned his attention was that of Teigh, Rutland (94).

Teigh church retains its medieval tower. The nave, rebuilt in 1782, is outside of the plainest Gothic imaginable and no particular architectural interest. Its interior, however, is remarkable for being arranged with three tiers of seats facing inwards, as in a college chapel, while at the west end the doorway is set in a composition which comprises the pulpit above and the reading-desk and clerk's desk to right and left, all with Gothic panelling and cusped and pinnacled canopies. The ribbed plaster

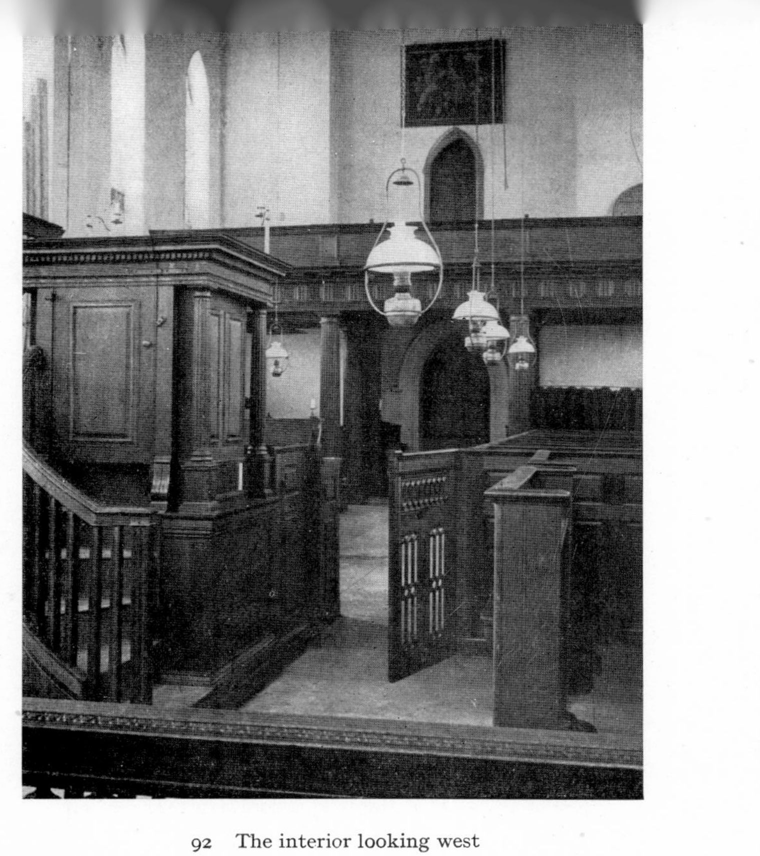

92 The interior looking west

93 Looking east from the gallery

Norton-by-Galby, Leicestershire, 1770, by Wing of Leicester
An unaltered interior retaining the central pulpit

94 Teigh, Rutland, 1782: the interior looking west

95 Stapleford, Leicestershire, 1783, by George Richardson

TWO OF THE EARL OF HARBOROUGH'S CHURCHES

ceiling is ornamented with escutcheons and the furnishings include a mahogany font on a brass bracket which pegs into the angle of the communion rails (135).

The Earl of Harborough's other Gothic church, which stands within the bounds of the park at Stapleford, was built shortly after that at Teigh. It is a considerably larger structure, and no part of the medieval church was retained. "Architect, Stavely of Melton," says Throsby, but "architect" here must mean builder, since an elevation of the church was exhibited at the Royal Academy in 1783 by George Richardson, best known as the author of a number of books of designs and editor of the two volumes of *The New Vitruvius Britannicus*. No doubt Richardson was the designer of Teigh and Saxby churches as well. Stapleford church has an oblong nave with slight transept-like projections, which contain the Sherard monuments, and a west tower, through the base of which lies the only entrance. The exterior of the nave is quite unencumbered by buttresses; the walls are surmounted by a solid parapet, with minute pinnacles, and adorned with a series of escutcheons exhibiting the alliances of the Earls of Harborough (83). (Among the attractions of Gothic were the facilities it offered for heraldic display.) The detail in general is much less realistic, regarded as an essay in medievalism, than the detail at Norton, or even at Croome, but the building as a whole is none the less charming for that. The interior, as at Teigh, is arranged on collegiate lines (95); to describe it, one more quotation from John Throsby, who wrote less than five years after its completion, may be permissible. "I entered the church," he says, "with much pleasure. It has one aisle, and neatly pewed with oak; the pews are ranged like a gallery on each side . . . . Here is no pulpit; the preacher teaches from a gallery at the west end of the aisle, where his Lordship and family sit . . . . This neat place of worship, which may long do honour to the Earl of Harborough's name, wants only some painted glass in the windows to give it an air of grandeur".

"Neat" Stapleford church, in common with most churches of its time, certainly is. That painted glass could have given it "an air of grandeur", in our eyes, is doubtful. But we can still admire the amenity of this spacious room, and examine with pleasure the reredos, "beautifully formed of marble, with borders of black, statuary, and dove colours" by Brown of Derby, and the Coade stone Gothic fireplace, with its relief of the sacrifice of Isaac, in the Earl's private gallery. And we may even regret that the original font, which was, we are told,[1] "a marble basin raised on a pillar, which will screw into the floor when wanted, but not to be stationary", is no more to be seen.

* * *

Other country churches in "the modern Gothic order" were built during the fifty years so far covered by this chapter. There is one at Werrington, Devon, dating from 1740—a very curious affair more closely related to the Gothic pavilions and temples with which the parks of the century were studded than to any other church; one at Preston-on-Stour,

[1] By J. Nichols, *op. cit.*

built for James West in 1752-7, with a highly ornate chancel; another of 1758 (but spoilt in 1871), at Rushock, Worcestershire; another, now deserted, at Bishopthorpe near York, built in 1766, probably to the design of Thomas Atkinson; another at Stanford-on-Teme, which dates from 1768 and has points in common with Croome; one of 1785 at Papplewick, Nottinghamshire; yet another at Teigngrace, Devon, built in 1787 but since deprived of its steeple and largely Victorianized. Nor is this list likely to be nearly complete. But it is time to glance at some Gothic town churches of the period.

The first shall be St. Nicholas', Warwick (96). The tower and spire of this church, replacing the medieval steeple, were built in 1748; the nave dates from 1779-80. It is generally stated that the designer of the steeple was one Johnson, and of the body of the church Job Collins. A few years back, however, there came to light in Sidbury, Worcester, a model of a Gothic church which is unmistakably St. Nicholas', Warwick; and a Thomas Johnson, architect, of whom nothing else is recorded, died in Sidbury in 1786. Obviously this Thomas Johnson was the owner of the model and the builder of St. Nicholas' spire, while the fact that the model represents the whole church, the nave of which is attributed to Job Collins, may be explained by the supposition that, when the time came for rebuilding the nave, Johnson had moved to Worcester and Collins was appointed to execute his design. And if that was so, one can understand how Francis Hiorn's design for the nave, which according to Field's *Warwick* (1815) was " far superior ", came to be rejected.

A point of interest about this model is that it is equipped with alternative spires, differing greatly in height and degree of ornamentation. The lower and simpler was built, and Field, as it happens, complains that the spire of St. Nicholas' is too low. Remembering the fate of the spire at Norton-by-Galby (91, 92, 93) we may consider that it was just as well—although, in fairness, it must be admitted that a number of perfectly stable high Gothic spires were built about this time.[1] Another point of interest is that the model was found in company with others, among which was the front of Warwick County Hall. And that, as noted above, was designed by Sanderson Miller and put up by the brothers Hiorn. Did Miller have something to do with this early Gothic Revival church?

The tower, sound in proportions and quite prettily detailed, is the best part of St. Nicholas'. The nave is as nearly square as makes no difference, with aisles divided off by clustered columns and plain plaster vaulting, not unlike that at Wicken; the chancel was enlarged in 1869. The single pyramidal roof which covers the whole nave is a remarkable piece of carpentry, but the cupola which crowns it makes a rather unhappy contribution to the external effect.

That a church should be Gothic without and Classical within seemed no anomaly in the eyes of the eighteenth century. There is such a church at Alcester, an early example in which the interior was rebuilt in 1729-33 by Edward and Thomas Woodward of Chipping Campden. In Bristol

[1] Nathaniel Wilkinson, of Worcester, rebuilt the spires of Ledbury, Ross, Mitcheldean and St. Andrew's, Worcester. John Cheshire, a native of Over Whitacre, rebuilt the spires of St. Martin's, Birmingham, St. Mary's, Leicester, and Hinckley.

96 St. Nicholas, Warwick: the steeple 1748, by Thomas Johnson; the nave 1779-80

97 St. Paul, Bristol, 1789-93, by Daniel Hague

St. Paul, Bristol

there were three—until the bombs came. Now there are only two, St. Michael's and St. Paul's; for the nave of St. Nicholas' is but the shell of itself, although its tower and spire stand unharmed. It is a serious loss.

St. Nicholas', Bristol, was built on the site of its medieval predecessor in 1762-8. The architect was a local man, James Bridges. The church cost more than £6,000, and we are told that it "brought a great charge upon the parish estates". Horace Walpole thought that it was "neat and truly Gothic", and the window tracery, indeed, is in a remarkably convincing Perpendicular. Nor could anyone complain about the height of the steeple—202 feet to the weathercock. But it was the interior of St. Nicholas', now utterly destroyed, that was its glory. In proportion it followed that form beloved of classical theorists, the double cube; in decoration it was "as perfectly Rococo as anything in England", with a particularly good plaster ceiling (by Thomas Stocking), in addition to an earlier reredos and a wrought-iron screen from the former church (131).

It is easy to see why the parishioners of St. Nicholas', in a city positively crowded with medieval churches, should have felt it incumbent on them to make the exterior of their new church Gothic. In the case of St. Michael's the same kind of argument was even more forcible, for when the old church was surveyed in 1774 the tower was found to be in reasonable condition and so, on the demolition of the rest of the fabric the following year, was allowed to stand. Thomas Paty, whom we noticed in the last chapter as father of William Paty, the architect of Christ Church, undertook to erect "a roomy elegant and commodious new Church" for between £1,800 and £2,000; subscriptions, including £300 from the Bristol Corporation and £150 from the Merchants' Hall, amounted to over £2,200; and the new church was opened in June 1777. Aesthetically, St. Michael's is not in the same class as St. Nicholas'. Nevertheless its interior, showing a combination of Doric columns and lintels with Gothic chancel arch and Gothic allusions in such details as the shallow panelling of the stonework, helps to illuminate for us the mentality of the age to which it belongs. One remembers the Doric joinery at Norton-by-Galby, and, further back, Gibbs's use of Doric to harmonize with the medieval tower at Derby. Gothic was felt to be rude yet solemn, and of the classical orders the Doric came nearest to possessing those qualities.

However, there is nothing rude or solemn in the interior of the third Bristol church of this group, St. Paul's (97, 98). Nor can the very tall columns that support its roof properly be classified as Doric. Indeed, it is not easy to classify them at all; Heath's *Bristol Guide* calls them "lofty pillars of stone, with fancied capitals", and perhaps that is good enough. St. Paul's was begun in 1789 and opened in 1795. Like St. Nicholas' it was an expensive proposition, and the parish had to pay a rate of 1s. 8d. in the pound for twenty years to meet the bill. At first it had been intended to build a classical church to a design by James Allen, the architect of St. Thomas's, but for some reason, probably dishonourable, this scheme was abandoned and a builder-architect called Daniel Hague was employed instead.[1] It seems that Hague's design

[1] See C. F. W. Dening, *The Eighteenth-century Architecture of Bristol.*

was based on sketches by a Rev. D. A. Small; the amateur was still a force in the Revival. Outside, this church with its 169 foot steeple possesses the stock characteristics of the Gothic of its time in an extreme degree. Judged by serious architectural standards, it is rather monstrous, but its scenic qualities are unquestionable and it is as a piece of romantic scenery that it must be judged.

St. Paul's, Bristol, has taken us to the end of the 1780's. But other Gothic town churches were built in the 'fifties, 'sixties and 'seventies. Among them were St. John's, Manchester (1769), St. Nicholas', Liverpool (1774)[1] and the parish churches of Stone (1754)[2], (90), Buckingham (1780), and Tetbury, Gloucestershire (100). The last is a remarkable building and merits consideration at length.

The full story of the events that led to the rebuilding of Tetbury church is a long one, not always creditable to those concerned, and it involves such familiar names as Francis Smith, Henry Flitcroft, and even James Gibbs. But here it is not necessary to look further back than 1777, when work began on the erection of the new church according to a design received two years earlier from Francis Hiorn.

The Hiorn family, of Warwick, have already figured in these pages more than once, and Francis, the son of David Hiorn, has been mentioned as architect of Tardebigge church and as having submitted a design for St. Nicholas', Warwick. Born in 1741 and dying in 1789, he seems to have had a great reputation as a Goth, and was employed to restore Arundel Castle; he also built a triangular tower in Arundel Park, and designed, but never built, a ruined castle for Nuneham Courtenay. He is known to have built one other Gothic church, at Stony Stratford in 1776. This is in many respects a cheaper and smaller version of Tetbury, but very bare outside; inside it has suffered at the hands of the nineteenth century. At Tetbury, Hiorn was both architect and builder. He received £3,658 16s. for building the church and £1,000 17s. for flooring and pewing it, in addition to the materials of the old fabric, which he valued at £400. The medieval tower was allowed to remain, and the new church was opened in 1781.

On plan the nave of Tetbury church is a simple parallelogram with passages running its full length outside the main walls and connecting with the interior by doors in each of the seven bays. A chancel of one bay projects to the east. Internally, the nave is divided up with false aisles by extremely thin piers of clustered shafts—actually wooden shells over iron cores—which branch out into plaster vaulting above (100). Round the three sides of the western half of the church is a gallery with Gothic-panelled front, and the whole is pewed in similar style. (The pulpit, however, did not survive certain alterations and additions made in 1901). What of its aesthetic qualities? There is no doubt as to what the eighteenth century thought about it. It was "thought to be equal, if not superior, to any Country Church in the Kingdom", we are told, and we catch a reflection of the critics' jargon of the time in an article by John Carter in the *Gentleman's Magazine* of 1802. "Upon what grounds,

[1] Architect, Joshua Brooker. Bombed.
[2] Architect, William Baker, designer of St. John's, Wolverhampton.

knowledge, or capability," Carter asks, "do some writers announce that the present church at Tetbury is a beautiful edifice of the first taste, and composed after the finest examples of our ancient edifices by imitations the most chaste and the most correct?"

Carter's question is purely rhetorical, for, with the assistance of a couple of thumbnail sections and a supply of theological banter, he had made it clear that his own opinion was very different. In the same series of articles he was equally sarcastic about Stony Stratford church, and it looks almost as if Carter had some special grudge against the harmless shade of Francis Hiorn. Perhaps he was embittered by a secret suspicion that his own Gothic, as exemplified in the chapel which he had built for John Milner at Winchester, was not really very different. But in 1947 we need not let archaeological pedantry come between us and Tetbury church. To us it may seem that the unbroken vistas of the lateral passages, to which Carter took exception, are justified as much by their drama as by their convenience. We are not offended when we recognize in the slender mouldings of the interior the same feeling for delicate linear pattern as that which informs the draperies of the Grecian ladies on the tablets adorning the walls. Nor do we expect from Hiorn any attempt at Gothic construction; the first stone-vaulted church of the Revival—St. Luke's, Chelsea—was forty years away in the future, and, since the taste of the time was for low relief in external architecture, there are no massive buttresses at Tetbury to pretend that the ceiling is of anything but plaster.

* * *

The period of the French wars was not very productive of churches of any sort. Of those which were built, probably a larger proportion than before were Gothic. The time had arrived when a Gothic church was no longer either a fashionable novelty or a calculated gesture of respect for the past; it was simply the obvious alternative to a classical church.

St. Alkmund's, Shrewsbury, may stand for the last decade of the eighteenth century. All but the tower of the former church on the site was demolished, somewhat unnecessarily, as the result of a panic caused by the collapse of the old St. Chad's in the same town. The present church dates from 1795. Its original fittings were victims of Victorian "restorers", but the fabric of this large aisleless hall in a thin Perpendicular style is still typical enough of its era. At the time of its opening it was, of course, highly praised. "It is to the taste of Messrs. Carline and Tilley that we are indebted for the Design of this beautiful Church," the *Shrewsbury Chronicle* noted, "and to their well-known skill and care in conducting every part of the execution; but more particularly to the Masonry; the Joiners' Work reflects the greatest credit upon Mr. John Hiram Haycock; and the plastering, by Mr. Joseph Bromfield, claims equal commendations. All the Iron Work was cast by the Coalbrook-Dale Company."

That the ironwork should be mentioned is significant. Cast iron was a most important addition to the Gothic designer's range of materials. To architects who could see nothing wrong in the standardization of

Gothic forms the ease and precision with which details could be repeated in cast iron must have seemed wholly desirable. It was particularly convenient for window tracery—and thus it was employed in St. Alkmund's. A prominent Goth of the period who specialized in its use for this purpose was William Porden. His *chef d'oeuvre* of domestic architecture, the second Eaton Hall, had cast-iron tracery throughout; and so had his church at Eccleston. The latter was designed in 1809 and pulled down just ninety years later. According to Ormerod, the Cheshire historian, it was to be "classed among the happiest imitations of Gothic architecture", although the iron tracery (in itself "elegant in design and beautifully executed") was "too slender when contrasted with the general proportions". We can judge for ourselves of the appearance of Eccleston church, and gauge the progress made in the first seventy years of the Gothic Revival, from a lithograph after J. C. Buckler, in which its pinnacles are displayed against that storm-laden sky with which, it would seem, the English climate in the early nineteenth century obliged the artists of "the Picturesque" so liberally (87).

99 Hartwell, Buckinghamshire, 1753-6, by Henry Keene: the south side of the interior

100

Tetbury, Gloucestershire, 1777-81, by Francis Hiorn: interior looking east (The screen dates from 1901)

101 St. George, Brandon Hill, Bristol, 1823
by Sir Robert Smirke

102 Ayot St. Lawrence, Hertfordshire, 1778-9
by Nicholas Revett

TWO GREEK DORIC PORTICOS

Chapter VI

THE REGENCY AND AFTER

THE meaning of the word Regency, applied as an adjective to the arts, is often stretched to cover a good deal more than was produced during the nine years when the future George IV was Regent. In the heading of this chapter, however, it is used as a noun in its strict historical sense, to denote the period which began with the Regency Act of 1811 and ended with George III's death in 1820. "And after", in a book called "Stuart and Georgian Churches", should, I suppose, mean "until George IV's death", i.e., until 1830. However, there is everything to be said, from our point of view, for the inclusion of William IV's reign in the Georgian period. For the accession of Queen Victoria and the break-up of the classical tradition form one of those rare coincidences which seem to have been specially arranged for the convenience of historians of architecture.

1811 is not in itself a year of great significance. The war was still on, and few churches were being built. Another seven years were to pass before Parliament appointed a Commission, with a million pounds to spend, to "examine the state of the parishes and extra parochial places in the metropolis and its vicinity, and other parts of England and Wales, to ascertain in which additional churches and chapels are most required, and the most effectual means of affording such accommodation", and thus initiated the most ambitious and widespread church building movement that had been seen in this country since the Reformation.

The churches built between the beginning of the Regency and the passing of the "Million Act" may be dealt with briefly. Two of the most important, on any count, were St. Luke's, Liverpool, and St. Michael's, Pitt Street, in the same city. Both were from the hand of John Foster, who had been a pupil of James Wyatt, had travelled in Greece with C. R. Cockerell, and became architect and surveyor to the Corporation of Liverpool. St. Luke's, a Gothic church, was designed as early as 1802, but not begun until 1810, while the tower was finished in 1831. One of the masters of *clichés* and trite quotations who contributed the text of Pyne's *Lancashire Illustrated* wrote of it: "As a chaste specimen of the decorative Gothic order, this church may vie with any similar erection in the kingdom; while its sublime character, so consistent with the uses to which it is appropriated, points it out to every feeling mind as one of those hallowed spots

'Where through the long-drawn aisle and fretted vault
The pealing anthem swells the note of praise'."

For a more recent estimate of its qualities Mr. John Summerson may be quoted: "It is a rather harsh Gothic building and the tower, in spite of much enrichment, is graceless and forbidding. The interior was notable for its timber columns and ingenious plasterwork".[1] The reader may take his choice ; indeed, there is not much else he can do, St. Luke's having been blitzed in 1941.

In the case of St. Michael's, Pitt Street, the basis for an original judgement no longer exists at all, because the church was bombed and then totally demolished. Begun in 1816, it was a classical building, in many respects modelled on St. Martin's-in-the-Fields. Unlike most of the earlier progeny of that famous church, it had a projecting Corinthian portico to the west. What was more, it had an immense porch with four columns at the *east* end—an unusual and rather grand feature of Foster's own devising. As one might guess, all this cost money. It cost more, in fact, than the parish of Liverpool, which had undertaken the erection of St. Michael's to provide a chapel of ease, could easily raise, with the result that in 1823, after £35,000 had already been spent, the completion of the building was handed over to the Liverpool Corporation. Its total cost was over £45,000—a figure which makes it perhaps the most expensive English church built outside London during the whole of our period.

St. Michael's, Pitt Street, was exceptional among the classical churches of the early nineteenth century in that it possessed a high steeple. In the majority of cases some sort of turret or cupola was all that was attempted. This was partly because of the obvious difficulty of combining any sort of tower with the predominantly horizontal *motifs* of Greek architecture—and by now every architect paid lip-service to Greek ideals, however odd his work would have looked if transported to Periclean Athens—partly because the Wren-Gibbs manner of steeple design was felt to be outmoded but no-one knew quite what to put in its place.

Traditionally a church had to have some sort of tower; also, one guesses, it must often have been thought desirable to give it one to distinguish it from the new dissenting house around the corner. Yet suitable Greek models were hard to come by. There were, in fact, only two with which much could be done—the Tower of the Winds and the choragic monument of Lysicrates. The best known adaptation of the former is seen in St. Pancras, London, whose steeple is composed of two imitations of it, one upon the other ; of the latter, one of the earliest is the miniature Portland stone version which rides on the roof of the brick and stucco church of St. John, Chichester, designed by James Elmes in 1812.

The towers and cupolas of Greek Revival churches proved a sitting target for the facetiousness of later, unsympathetic generations, for sugar-castors and pepper-pots were images which occurred readily to the Victorian mind. Their porticos, on the other hand, have a dignity which no one has been able to deny. The worst that can be said of a portico is that it is " gloomy", but this in England is as much a criticism of the climate as of the architecture. The chief contemporary criticism of church porticos was that they were expensive; one of the great recommendations of Gothic, in the view of the Commissioners for the New Churches, was that since it did not require these costly appendages it was cheaper. Still, plenty of porticos were built, both before

[1] *The Bombed Buildings of Britain*, edited by J. M. Richards, 1942.

103 Dodington, Gloucestershire, 1803, by James Wyatt
From a drawing by J. C. Buckler in the possession of Mrs. Mango

104 A new church for Tyringham, Buckinghamshire, designed c.1796, by Sir John Soane but never built

105 Markham Clinton, Nottinghamshire, 1833, by Sir Robert Smirke

106 St. Andrew, Hove, 1824-6, by Sir Charles Barry

and after the "Million Act". St. Paul's, Worthing, designed by Rebecca, has a bold example of 1812; so as not to conflict with it, the cupola is compressed to the merest knob. St. David's, Exeter, designed by James Green in 1816, had another; this church no longer exists but is worth illustrating because with its oblong nave, west portico and cupola it is so thoroughly representative of what was to be a standard type of church for the next fifteen or twenty years (109).

Gothic churches might not need porticos, but their towers presented their designers with no difficulties at all; one imagines that the money saved from Grecian porticos must often have been spent on Gothic towers. A more real advantage of Gothic was that, although strict symmetry was always preserved, the plan of a Gothic church did not necessarily have to be forced into the temple formula which, in spite of the departures in the direction of more varied planning made during the latter part of the eighteenth century, had become *de rigueur* with the general acceptance of the authority of Greece. St. Thomas's, Dudley (113), is an ambitious example of a pre-Commissioners Gothic church with a non-rectangular plan. A rebuilt parish church (not a chapel of ease), it was designed in 1817 and erected in Bath stone at a cost of £24,000; the architect was William Brooks, whose best known building was the London Institution.[1] On plan the outside walls of the body of the church form an unequal-sided octagon, longer from east to west than from north to south. The clustered columns of the nave are set out in the same figure, but with the shorter sides of the octagon reduced in length, so that the orientation of the building is more clearly expressed internally than externally; there is no real chancel but merely a shallow sanctuary balancing the space taken up by the organ at the west end. Abutting the west wall is a high tower surmounted by a spire, with a total height of 175 feet. The style is Perpendicular, as was that of the majority of Gothic churches of the time. There are ambiguities in the design—the large central windows in the north and south sides are in no way indicative of the internal arrangements—and the detail is coarse, mechanical and archaeologically quite unconvincing. Nevertheless, the church as a whole is a spirited performance and has an undeniably romantical silhouette.

* * *

The Act of 1711 that provided for the building of "Queen Anne's churches" was avowedly designed as a means "for redressing the inconveniences and growing mischiefs" arising from the increase of Dissenters and Papists. In 1818, when the Church Building Act that resulted in the Commissioners' Churches became law, the circumstances were such as to cause churchmen even more concern than their great-grandfathers had had reason to feel. The threat of popery, it was true, could no longer be taken very seriously. But among the rapidly growing populations of London and the industrial towns Dissent was rampant, and to it was added another enemy of the Establishment, more formidable

[1] Classical; demolished in 1936. Rickman in his diary records going to see St. Thomas's, Dudley; he thought that Brooks's Gothic was not up to his Grecian, with which judgment one may concur.

than either of the older ones—active atheism. A writer in the *Quarterly Review* in 1820 describes the situation as he and others of his way of thinking saw it: "The speculative impiety which has long existed in this country is no longer contented, as in the days of Chubb and Collins, to rest in speculation; it has produced a system of practical immorality; and as in colonial wars the perilous practice has sometimes been resorted to of proclaiming freedom to all slaves who will take up arms against their owners, so in the war which the preachers of this philosophy have declared against the civil and religious institutions of society, the bounty which they hold out to their deluded disciples is an immediate emancipation from all the restraints which the laws of God impose upon the selfish and sinful propensities of man. The populace are told in plain terms that religion is a mere juggle between priests and kings, for the purpose of keeping them in subjection; that men are like the beasts that perish; and that, as they have no other world to look for, they are fools if they refrain from any gratification which this can give them, or suffer any prejudices to stand in the way of their interest and their inclination."

To counteract such tendencies more churches obviously were necessary. Even if it could not be allowed that religion was invented to keep the populace in subjection, every good constitutionalist, in the face of the results of democracy conjoined with impiety (both speculative and practical) abroad, had to recognize that it had an incidental usefulness in keeping it in order. Besides, some national gesture was called for to signalize the victorious ending of the war with France—and what more suitable than the erection of a couple of hundred churches? The question was above party, and the bill went through without real opposition.

During the whole of the period with which this book is concerned—and until 1843, to be precise—the parish was a civil as well as an ecclesiastical unit, and an Act of Parliament was required before a new parish could be formed. The Act of 1818, however, provided that for ecclesiastical purposes any parish might, with the consent of the bishop and the patron of the church, and subject to the approval of the King in council, be divided into two or more separate parishes. Such division was not to take effect completely until after the death, resignation, or avoidance of the existing incumbent. Similarly, a parish might be divided into ecclesiastical districts in cases where division into separate parishes was not thought expedient. The Commissioners appointed to administer the Act were empowered to make grants, out of the million pounds put at their disposal, for building churches or chapels in parishes containing not less than 4,000 persons and not having church accommodation for more than 1,000, or in parishes where 1,000 or more of the inhabitants were living more than four miles from any church or chapel. The application for new churches had to come from the parishes and had to be sanctioned by the majority of the inhabitants who were assessed for the poor-law rate—or, in the case of parishes under the care of a select vestry or body, by four-fifths of that body and at the same time by two-thirds *in value* of the proprietors of land. When the Commissioners were satisfied that a parish was unable to bear any part of the cost of the new church, they might grant the whole sum necessary. Otherwise, an

107 Theale, Berkshire, 1820-30, by Edward Garbett
An ambitious effort in " the lancet style "

108 Christchurch, Meadow Lane, Leeds, 1823-6, by R. D. Chantrell
A typical northern Commissioners' church

109 St. David, Exeter, 1816, by James Green Demolished 1897

agreed proportion would be raised by the parish, through rates or subscriptions, or both, and the Commissioners would grant the balance and perhaps advance part of the sum due from the parish as a loan. Other clauses prohibited intra-mural burial, except in vaults wholly arched with brick or stone and reached by steps outside the walls, and stipulated that one fifth of the sittings in each church must be free. The rents of the remainder of the seats were to be fixed by the Commissioners, and from them provision was to be made for the minister and clerk.

The Commissioners' churches have come in for criticism ever since they were built; odious comparisons with the churches erected under the Act of 1711 were inevitable from the first. It must be admitted that some of this criticism is justified. The necessity of designing every church to hold as large a congregation as possible was a part of the programme not conducive to good architecture. The emphasis in general was on quantity rather than quality, and many of the churches built by the Commissioners were cheap—the cost of the larger churches usually worked out at something around £8 per head of the congregation they could hold—and some were nasty. Nevertheless, the best of them are fit to be set beside the best secular architecture of the time.

* * *

In the following pages no important object would be served by going out of our way to distinguish in every case between the Commissioners' churches and those built under other auspices. Architecturally, there is no real dividing line. Yet it will be as well, perhaps, to glance at a few Commissioners' churches first.

Among the architects most employed by the Commissioners in the provinces was Francis Goodwin. Born at King's Lynn in 1784, Goodwin is one of the typical architects of the age. He has been mentioned earlier for his addition of steeples to St. Paul's, Birmingham, and St. Peter's, Manchester. These were both classical efforts, and Goodwin's best known building, the old Manchester Town Hall, was also classical. But Goodwin, in common with many of his contemporaries, was a practitioner—not to beg the question by calling him a master—of more styles than one. Towards the end of his life he published a book of villa designs which include a number of Italian examples. And most of his churches are Gothic. This is an additional reason for selecting Goodwin as representative, for of the 214 churches built by the Commissioners 174 were in Gothic of one sort or another.

Goodwin's own special brand of Gothic can with a little practice be easily recognized, even from a distance; he liked fat pinnacles and lean towers. He also liked cast iron tracery, and was evidently not at all put out by the contrast of its slenderness with the more robust proportions of his masonry detail. Most of his churches stand in the towns of the Midlands and North-west, although one of the earliest was St. Paul's, Portsmouth. A busy man, he worked out his own formula for a Commissioners' church and then proceeded to repeat it, with such modifications as his fancy or the money at his disposal dictated, until he—or was it his clients ?—grew tired of it. Thus his Portsmouth church and churches by him at Birmingham, Kidderminster, and West Bromwich (all begun in 1820 or 1821) formed a group which so far as their interiors were concerned differed only in dimensions and detail. Outside they are more readily distinguishable mainly because two of them, Kidderminster and West Bromwich, have towers of differing design, while the others have none.

The problem of equipping a Gothic church with a sufficiently imposing west front was one which, as we shall see, could worry Charles Barry. In the group of churches mentioned, Goodwin solved it in his own way. Denied the projecting portico of classicism, he resorted to the use of a recessed *motif* instead, scooping out of his west fronts triplets of lofty, cavernous portals. Perhaps he got the idea from Peterborough cathedral, but whatever his inspiration may have been the result is certainly a success. This was evidently recognized by Goodwin's contemporaries. Thomas Rickman noted in his diary on June 24, 1826, " I looked at West Bromwich, which is not yet going on again : it seems as if its front would be one of the best of Goodwin's ". This was generous of Rickman, because he had himself competed unsuccessfully for this church.

Originally none of the four churches in this group had internal arcades ; nor had they chancels. All of them were of Bath stone and all had built out vestries attached to the east end, large circular windows with cast-iron tracery of identical design above the altar, plaster ceilings, and galleries. William Smith, in his *County of Warwick*, describes Holy Trinity, Birmingham (115, 116), at some length, and gives us a fair idea of the features the average late Georgian spectator admired in such a church. " On entering the interior," we are informed, " the visitor is struck with the beauty of the large circular window, glazed with painted glass ; the altar-piece, by Foggo, representing Christ healing at the pool of Bethesda ; the height of the ceiling ; and the chaste yet magnificent appearance of the etched glass with which the windows are glazed. The pulpit and desk are placed just without the altar, one on each side ; they are of similar form, and, as well as the pews, are of deal, painted and grained to resemble oak . . . . The ceiling is in character with the exterior, judiciously ornamented with groined ribs, bosses &c., and from its height gives an idea of air and ventilation which the flat ceilings of the Grecian style seem to deny. Galleries, supported by cast iron pillars, representing small clustered columns, occupy the west end and north and south sides, in the first of which is a beautiful Gothic organ designed by the same architect." Fortunately Holy Trinity, Birmingham, has not been so much altered as to lose all its original character and is well worth a visit. But the most spectacular exterior of the group, gaining a good deal, it is true, from its setting, is that of Kidderminster.

Among the other Gothic churches designed by Goodwin for the Commissioners were St. Matthew's, Walsall (1820) and St. George's, Hulme (1826). The former is remarkable for its lavish Tudor Gothic plaster ceiling, with heavy ornamental pendants, over the nave ; the latter, sadly begrimed now by the soot of Manchester, is a very large and showy church with a western tower, burgeoning in an even more extravagant crop of pinnacles than is usual in Goodwin's designs.

On one of the plates in Pyne's *Lancashire Illustrated*, which has been quoted earlier in this chapter, engravings of two Manchester churches are set side by side. One is St. George's, Hulme, the other St. Matthew's, Campfield. To compare them (or better still to compare the two churches themselves) is to realize the shortcomings of Goodwin's Gothic, skilful and efficient in its way though it is. For St. Matthew's was manifestly designed by an architect who possessed one quality which played no great part in Goodwin's Gothic churches—sensibility. That architect's name was Charles Barry.

Barry's greatest work, the Houses of Parliament at Westminster, marked the end of the most critical phase in the Battle of the Styles. But while the plan and general conception of that vast agglomeration of late Perpendicular was Barry's own, practically all its detail proceeded from the fertile brain of Augustus Welby Pugin. Barry's early churches, on the other hand, show him playing the Goth without the advantage of Pugin's assistance. They were admired when they were new, and the architect's son tells us that his letters show that he regarded them with "complacency". But this complacency was, he adds, "destined to undergo a woeful change in after years, when these churches served as a continual subject of laughter to his friend Mr. Pugin and to himself". (Barry "used to retaliate by reference to Mr. Pugin's early work at Windsor Castle"). Certainly they are no more correct, archaeologically, than the generality of the Gothic churches of the day. But correctness is not everything—or for that matter as much as the later Barry and Victorian critics believed.

Barry's son says that his father "in spite of his admiration for the horizontal lines and regular forms of Egyptian and Greek architecture, entered so thoroughly into the vertical principle of Gothic, that he felt unsatisfied in carrying out any Gothic building without a spire." At Manchester he had his own way in the matter. But it was a matter of lasting regret to him that he was not allowed to add a spire to the tower of St. Peter's, Brighton (110), the most important of his Gothic churches, which he designed a year later than St. Matthew's, in 1823.

Of St. Peter's, Brighton, the younger Barry writes: "The opportunity was considerable; the competition exceedingly severe, and his victory was a subject of great delight and encouragement to him." Later in life, when Pugin's magic influence had come between Barry and his youth, he "felt dissatisfied with the faults of detail and the mixture of styles admitted therein; and his architectural conscience felt a strong and characteristic repugnance to the aisle windows, on the ground that, being in one height, they sinned against 'truth' in giving no indication of the galleries within". The galleries have since been removed, and so has Barry's polygonal apse; the present chancel was added by G. Somers Clarke in 1906. So far as the exterior was concerned, Barry conceived his church in the first place as a grand termination to the north end of the Steyne. An impressive west—or rather south—front was thus necessary, and, to quote Barry's son once more, "the fronts of churches appeared to him deficient in extension". To overcome this difficulty Barry encased the lower part of the tower with screen walls heavily buttressed at the corners, the buttresses being connected to the real tower by fliers. This device gave the front the extra extension he desired, and at the same time allowed him to express the "vertical principle of Gothic" in a dramatically lofty arch without weakening the main structure. As one contemplates the Portland stone mass of St. Peter's, gleaming in the clear Brighton air, one may feel grateful to Barry for the boldness of his vision. But it is hard to see how a spire (on which the architect's heart was so firmly set that he made a design as late as 1841) could have failed to spoil matters.

* * *

Barry's success with St. Peter's brought him other commissions in the Brighton neighbourhood. The only one which concerns us here is that which resulted in St. Andrew's (formerly the Brunswick chapel), Hove (106, 121). This was designed in 1824, for a Dr. Everard, and completed in 1826. It is not a large building, but it is none the less a landmark in the history of English architecture. For here, for the first time, Barry worked in that Italian Renaissance style for which, after the Houses of Parliament, he is best known to posterity. Of the introduction of this style Mr. John Summerson has written: "All the young men who went abroad after Waterloo seem to have been struck with the idea of giving Vicenza a rest and looking, for a change, towards the churches and palaces of Rome, Venice and Florence. Barry was extraordinarily quick and shrewd in his perceptions and won by a head in the race to exploit the new discoveries."[1]

Appreciation of how novel the Brunswick chapel must have appeared to Georgian eyes does not make any inordinate demand on the historical sense. For the west front of this little church has a freshness which the years have not withered nor custom staled. Severe critics may discover faults of detail, but a slight *gaucherie* is not without charm when the sensibility of a Barry underlies it. The interior is today of small interest, for an overdesigned chancel was added by Charles Barry junior in 1882, and the altarpiece, which was the chief feature of the interior as his father left it, disappeared in the process.

Although the first building of the Italian movement was thus a church, its later phases were almost entirely secular. With a very few exceptions, among which C. R. Cockerell's Holy Trinity, Clifton, (1829) was perhaps the most notable, every church built during the dozen years preceding Queen Victoria's accession was Gothic or Greek—with the comparative graph rising steadily in favour of Gothic. (An insignificant Romanesque revival, heralded as early as 1815 by Thomas Hakewill's church at Old Wolverton, Buckinghamshire, may be included under the head of Gothic).

Of the architects who designed Grecian churches for the Commissioners in the provinces Robert Smirke is perhaps the best known. Born in 1780, Smirke built his first church, St. Nicholas', Strood, in 1814. This is a plain, utilitarian building, and Smirke was not really happy unless he had a portico to play with—although "play" is perhaps not a word to be associated with the solemn and conscientious architecture of the designer of the British Museum. He was one of the Board of Works architects

[1] *Georgian London*, 1945, p.233.

110 St. Peter, Brighton, 1823-8, by Sir Charles Barry

111 St. Thomas. Stockport, Cheshire, 1825, by George Basevi

112 St. Leonard. Bilston, Staffordshire, 1826, by Francis Goodwin

who acted as advisers to the Commissioners, and the only one of the three —the other two were Nash and Soane—to build anything for that body outside the metropolitan area. Most of his churches belong to the oblong porticoed type, and he was as repetitive in Greek as Goodwin was in Gothic. Thus St. George's, Brandon Hill, Bristol (101), built in 1823, is virtually a duplicate St. James's, Hackney. It has a quadrastyle Doric portico with a cupola behind it and a spacious but empty interior with a flat ceiling and galleries supported by Doric columns. It is handsome enough in its way, and well built—but hardly inspired. St. Philip's, Salford, (which is duplicated by All Saints', Wyndham Place) follows a less usual plan. In this case a western portico was ruled out by the necessity of the church presenting its showiest side to the south. So to St. Philip's Smirke gave a semicircular porch, with six columns of his favourite order, the Ionic, projecting from the centre of the south front. Above this rises a high steeple, consisting of a cylindrical belfry, with a peristyle, surmounted by a cupola, which might have come from almost any of Smirke's other churches. The interior, which is about sixty feet wide, has galleries supported by square pillars with elongated Doric columns rising from their fronts up to the flat ceiling. St. Philip's is today known in Manchester as " the flat iron". That is not really fair and, questions of aesthetics aside, Smirke did at any rate give the Mancunians and the Commissioners their money's worth, providing accommodation for 1,828 worshippers for the moderate sum of £14,000.

Not all Smirke's churches, however, were designed with the need for economy high on the programme. At Markham Clinton, in Nottinghamshire (105), there is a small country church in which we may see him unfettered by such considerations. It was built in 1833 for the Duke of Portland, and it belongs to the class of " sepulchral churches " whose popularity with the great landowners we have noted in an earlier chapter. Its plan is cruciform, with an octagonal tower rising from a square podium at the junction and a four-column Doric portico to the east ; under the tower is a circular vestibule and the arms of the cross contain oblong burial chapels. Detail throughout, with the exception of the dome which crowns the tower, is severely Greek, and all is solidly carried out in stone— as Smirke's buildings nearly always are. There is something peculiarly touching about this Attic outpost on its ridge near the Great North Road, but some of its charm is no doubt due to the adventitious qualities contributed by age and by the gentle process of decay.[1]

Although Sir John Soane himself never built a church outside London, there is at least one which can only be described as Soanic. St. Andrew's, Plymouth, was designed in 1823 by John Foulston, who was responsible for so much of that town's Georgian magnificence. " Its character ", Foulston tells us in his *Public Buildings in the West of England*, " is intended to be severely Greek, not abounding, but choice in ornament." Most people would hesitate to call St. Andrew's "severely" anything, and the incised lines with which its Dartmoor granite front is adorned

[1] St. Paul's, Nottingham, which would appear to have been the only church built by William Wilkins, had a Doric portico and a tower very like that of Markham Clinton. It was built in 1822 and demolished a century later.

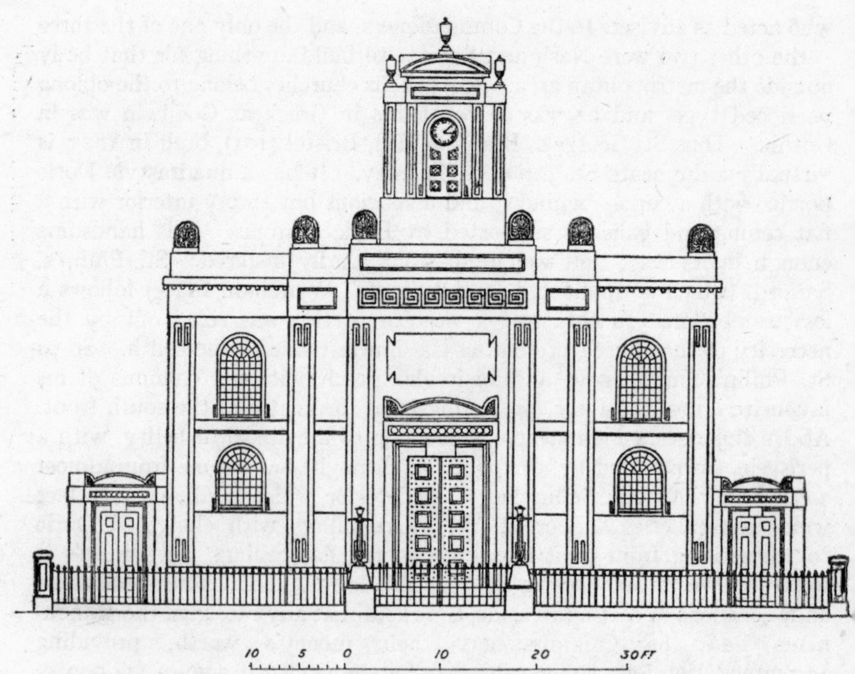

St. Andrew's Plymouth, 1823, by John Foulston: west elevation The clock tower was never built (From Foulston's *Public Buildings in the West of England*)

originated at a source nearer home than fifth-century Athens; this kind of ornament constituted Soane's chief contribution to the vernacular of the time. But the total sum of Foulston's debt to Sir John becomes apparent only when one studies the elevation of the church in Foulston's book. For the clock turret which there unifies the design, but which unfortunately was never built, is clearly based on the upper part of the mausoleum attached to Dulwich College picture gallery, which Soane had designed some twelve years before. Within, there is again more than a trace of Soane in the much flattened chancel arch, but the Egyptian columns supporting the galleries could only have been designed by the architect of the Oddfellows Hall at Devonport. Originally there was a central three-decker of exceptional splendour.

Although Soane's own very individual style was not often imitated, the indirect influence of his personality, transmitted through the medium of his many pupils, was great. Smirke himself had worked in his office—for a short time; Soane had no great opinion of Smirke's abilities. But of all the men who had passed through Soane's hands the most talented was George Basevi, who went to him in 1810 and left him for three years travel in Italy and Greece in 1816. Basevi's most famous building is the Fitzwilliam Museum at Cambridge, which, owing to his fatal fall from the western tower of Ely cathedral, he did not live to see completed. For the Commissioners he built two churches, St. Mary's, Greenwich, and St. Thomas's, Stockport (111). The former has been pulled down, but the Stockport church, which dates from 1825, still stands. At Greenwich

113 St. Thomas, Dudley, Worcestershire, 1817, by William Brooks

114 Ombersley, Worcestershire, 1825-9, by Thomas Rickman and Henry Hutchinson: the north arcade, showing Rickman's solution of the gallery problem in a Gothic church

115 The east end

116 The interior, looking east

Holy Trinity, Bordesley, Birmingham, 1823, by Francis Goodwin

117 Hartlebury, Worcestershire, 1836-7, by Thomas Rickman

118 Stoke Doyle, Northamptonshire, 1722

119 Patshull, Staffordshire, 1742, by James Gibbs

120 St. Peter, Brighton, 1823, by Sir Charles Barry

121 St. Andrew, Hove, 1824, by Sir Charles Barry

FOUR DOORWAYS

Basevi combined a tower and west portico in the usual fashion. Evidently he was not satisfied with this arrangement, for at Stockport he placed the tower at the west end and the portico at the east. The church thus follows the general plan of Hawksmoor's church of St. Alphege, Greenwich, with which Basevi may have become familiar during his visits to the site of St. Mary's. Indeed, it seems possible that Basevi at this time was an admirer of Hawksmoor's work in general; a writer in the *Gentleman's Magazine* in 1829 said of the tower of St. Mary's, Greenwich, that "it must strike every observer as an imitation of the pinnacled towers of the old English style". This, in spite of the fact that its detail was entirely Greek; is not the nearest parallel to be found in the towers of St. Anne's, Limehouse, and St. George's-in-the-East? St. Thomas's, Stockport, is as a whole very much the kind of church one can imagine Hawksmoor would have built had he lived in the days of the Greek Revival. The high tower planted firmly on the ground and after eighty feet or so of Grecian severity blossoming into a clock stage and cupola of fantastic silhouette, the Corinthian *antae* at the angles of the nave, the ample Ionic portico to the east—these features combine to produce a church quite unlike any other of its period, and at the same time original in the deeper sense. The interior, too, is out of the ordinary. Not only are the lesser details distinguished, but the colonnades over the galleries manage for once to be something more than rows of glorified ceiling-props.

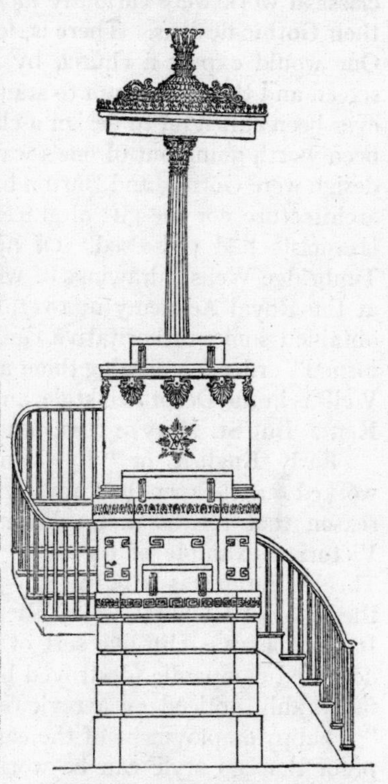

Three-decker pulpit originally at St. Andrew's Plymouth, 1823: designed by John Foulston (From *Public Buildings in the West of England*)

* * *

Basevi was by no means the only architect at this time who was susceptible to the spell of the native baroque of a hundred years earlier. One of the most striking examples of the influence of the latter is provided by Normanton Park church, Rutland, whose tower, designed by the elder Thomas Cundy and executed by his son in 1826, exactly reproduces the towers of Thomas Archer's Westminster church, St. John's, Smith Square. But the time has come to bid farewell to classicism and return to the Gothic movement, which held so much for the future, both of good and of evil.

The average Gothic church of the 'twenties and 'thirties is not an attractive building. Architects capable of refinement and elegance in classical work were curiously incapable of transferring those qualities to their Gothic designs. There is, for example, the case of Decimus Burton. One would expect a church by the designer of the Hyde Park Corner screen and the Athenæum to stand out from the ruck. And had Burton ever been called on to design a classical church, it would, no doubt, have been worth going out of one's way to see. But the churches that he did design were Gothic, and Burton had neither an understanding of medieval architecture nor the gift of graceful parody that an earlier generation of classicists had possessed. Of his most elaborate effort, Holy Trinity, Tunbridge Wells, (drawings of which he considered worthy of exhibition at the Royal Academy in 1827) it has been said that he seems to have obtained some authoritative Gothic details and then treated them as a formal "order", enlarging them up to the scale of the church. Tunbridge Wells is in the Decorated style, and so is Burton's church at Southborough, Kent. But St. Mary's, Riverhead, in the same county, is Early English.

Early English, or "the Lancet style", had the advantage that it worked out cheaper than anything else. But it was not always for that reason that it was used. What is probably the most ambitious pre-Victorian example of its use is to be seen at Theale, Berkshire (107). Theale church was built in 1820-32 at the sole expense of the patroness of the living of Tilehurst, a Mrs. Sheppard; its designer was Edward Garbett. It is a massive, cliff-like sort of building, with a tower copied from the detached campanile (destroyed by Wyatt) at Salisbury. In 1822 it was favourably noticed by a reviewer in the *Quarterly*, who described it as "a happy employment of the early or lancet Gothic, (which) affords full proof that no style can be worked more easily or with better effect." Nevertheless, the Lancet style never became really popular. Perpendicular or Decorated, or something combining features of both, was the rule. The names of most of the Gothicists of the eighteen-twenties and 'thirties are preserved in the pages of the Architectural Publication Society *Dictionary of Architecture*, but hardly anywhere else. One of the most prolific was Peter Atkinson, who built a large number of churches in Yorkshire. Between 1819 and 1828 Atkinson had as partner his former pupil Richard Hey Sharp; among the joint designs were St. Mark's, Woodhouse, Leeds, (1823) and Scarborough new church (1826). Another northern partnership was that of Woodhead and Hurst, who were responsible for St. George's, Sheffield (1821). Then there was J. Taylor, who designed Christ Church, Bradford (since replaced) as early as 1815, and, later on, the churches of Attercliffe-cum-Darnal, Sheffield (1822), and St. Mary, Quarry Hill, Leeds (1823). The architect of St. Mary, Sheffield (1826) was J. Potter, of Lichfield. Gothic early obtained a great numerical preponderance over Classic in the north, so that these northern churches constitute something like a regional development. Christ Church, Leeds (108), begun in 1823, is illustrated here as an example of the class. Tall and lean, its exterior, at any rate, is not devoid of a certain drama—which emerges more clearly, however, in early steel engravings, showing its tower rising in the background of a romanticized industrial landscape, than in the drab reality of its present-day surroundings. Its designer was R. D. Chantrell, who had spent seven years in Soane's office, and who at the very beginning of the Victorian era was to rebuild Leeds parish church.

Of the lesser known architects who built Gothic churches south of the Trent, Thomas Plowman should be mentioned. If we are to believe the A.P.S. *Dictionary*, which states that he died in 1828 at the age of twenty-one, Plowman was one of the few infant prodigies of architecture, entering the King's College, Cambridge, competition when he was sixteen and building his one recorded church at nineteen. The latter stands at Churchill, Oxfordshire; its tower is a reproduction of Magdalen tower, reduced a third in size, and the roof of its nave is a starved version of the roof of Christ Church hall. Then there was John Pinch, whose Hungerford church was begun before Waterloo and who at Bathwick managed to capture something of the richness of fifteenth-century Somerset work. A later West Country church whose architect seems to have been sensitive to the *genius loci* is St. Mary's, Penzance, designed by Charles Hutchins in 1834. St. Michael's, Stamford, by John Brown of Norwich, may be chosen to round off this paragraph, its date being 1836.

But the churches of the most important Gothicist of pre-Victorian days are yet to be considered. Thomas Rickman is best remembered today as the nomenclator of the English Gothic styles. For generations the terms "Early English", "Decorated", and "Perpendicular", as first advanced in Rickman's *Attempt to Discriminate the Styles of English Architecture* (1819), have seemed to possess rather the same sort of inevitability as the names of the months or days of the week. They are arbitrary and slightly absurd terms, when one comes to think about them, but perhaps those very qualities have recommended them to the English mind, in preference to the straightforward decimal system (as it were) of First, Second and Third Pointed. And if the system is typically English so, in its curious unpredictability, was the career of its inventor. Of Quaker stock, Rickman was trained for medicine but became a clerk in an insurance broker's office. At the age of thirty-three he began to study and sketch medieval churches. Three years later he was elected professor of architecture at the Liverpool Academy, and soon afterwards, without any training in our sense of the word, set up on his own as an architect. In spite of his active membership of the Society of Friends (which, characteristically enough, he eventually left to join the ritualistic Irvingites) he was very widely employed in building churches for the Establishment. His diaries, covering the greater part of his working life, are preserved at the Royal Institute of British Architects; in one entry he is attending Meeting, in the next corresponding with a bishop.

Early editions of Rickman's celebrated book begin with diagrams of the classical orders ("as a peace-offering to the shade of Vitruvius", Eastlake remarks), and several of his churches are Grecian. The most remarkable of these was St. Thomas's, Edgbaston, of which only the tower and the west front with its quadrant Ionic colonnades survived the bombs. It was a huge church, and could hold a congregation of 2,125; what remains is sufficiently impressive. It dated from 1825-7, as does also St. Peter's, Dale End, Rickman's Doric church in the same city. But several years earlier, in St. George's, Birmingham, Rickman had set a new standard in medieval scholarship applied to church architecture.

Charles Eastlake, the nineteenth-century historian of the Gothic Revival, criticized St. George's at length. After lamenting the fact that the window tracery, though " remarkably good in motive ", was executed in cast iron, he noted that " no other structural meanness is observable in other parts of the building. The walls are of fair thickness, stouter indeed than those in some of Pugin's churches. The tower, especially in its upper part, is well designed ; and but for the rigidly formal arrangement of its subordinate features, the west end would have been an effective composition. Internally, the nave arches have a bolder span, and the aisle windows are splayed more deeply than was usual in contemporary work ".

During the eighteen-twenties, when Rickman was busiest designing churches, he had as partner Henry Hutchinson, a young man of talent, if not of genius, who died before his time. It is not always possible to tell what is Rickman's and what Hutchinson's work. Among the most important products of the partnership were the churches of St. Peter's, Preston, Hampton Lucy, Warwickshire, Ombersley, Worcestershire and Christ Church, Coventry, all begun between 1821 and 1830. In the Preston church, built for the Commissioners, Rickman dared to depart from the strict symmetry that is one of the most obvious and most un-Gothic characteristics of the majority of the churches of the period (not excepting most of Rickman's own) by placing the steeple at the north-west corner of the nave. At Coventry he found a magnificent fourteenth-century steeple ready-made ; the church he added to it has been blitzed. But in many ways the two country churches are the most interesting of the four. Hampton Lucy, which was begun in 1822, is a very rich late-decorated effort (equipped with an even richer French-looking chevet by Sir Gilbert Scott). Ombersley, like St. Peter's, Preston, has a spire with flying buttresses. It also has a spacious chancel, and the window tracery for once is not of the same pattern throughout the church. Inside, there are quite convincing arcades and realistic roof-bosses ; the galleries, following Rickman's usual and sensible scheme, are kept well back from the arcades, within the aisles (114). The detail generally is without question rather thin. But it is also firm and crisp, and if one would take the measure of Rickman as a church architect, Ombersley is the place to visit. Certainly it gives a more favourable idea of his powers than the church at nearby Hartlebury (117), which, although ten years later in date, contains within a curiously disjointed exterior slender piers and plaster vaults which recall the eighteenth-century Gothic of Tetbury.

On Rickman's position in the history of English architecture Eastlake shall be given the last word. " His churches ", he writes, " are perhaps the first of that period in which the details of old work were reproduced with accuracy of form. Up to this time antiquaries had studied the principles of medieval architecture, and to some extent classified the phases through which it had passed, while architects had indirectly profited by their labours when endeavouring to imitate in practice the works of the Middle Ages. Rickman united both functions in one man.

122 Detail of screen, the Palace chapel, Bishop Auckland, County Durham

123 The pulpit, Abbey Dore, Herefordshire, 1634

124 Detail of screen, Ingestre, Staffordshire, 1676

125 Honington, Warwickshire, c.1690

126 Ingestre, Staffordshire, 1676

127 Castle Bromwich, Warwickshire, 1731

THREE PULPITS

He had examined the best examples of Gothic with the advantage of technical information. He did his best to design it after the advantage of personal study. In the science of his art he will not, of course, bear comparison with Willis. In the analysis of its general principles he must yield to Whewell. In capability of invention he ranks, even for his time, far below Pugin. But it may be fairly questioned whether, if we consider him in the twofold capacity of a theorist and a practitioner, he did not do greater service to the cause than either his learned contemporaries or his enthusiastic disciple."

"The cause"—in those two words resides the justification for this book's ending where it does. Gothic architecture in the second half of the eighteenth century had been a side-show, while classicism held the centre of the arena. In the first third of the nineteenth it was an alternative act, which most good classicists could put on when it was expected of them. But for the Victorian the Gothic Revival was a Cause. If any one man could be held responsible for the change, that man was Augustus Welby Pugin. *Contrasts in Architecture,* Pugin's first and most telling polemic, appeared in 1836. Nothing in the least like it had been seen before. No "peace offerings to the shade of Vitruvius" here, but a burning conviction that Gothic was the true, the only architecture—at any rate for churches built by Christian Englishmen. And the Christian Englishmen, oddly enough, before long found that they agreed, almost to a man. But that is another story.

Chapter VII

CRAFTSMEN AND ARTISTS

AFTER one of the less circumstantial biographies in his *Anecdotes of Painting in England* Horace Walpole remarks : " The reader must excuse such brief or trifling articles. This work is but an essay towards the history of our arts : all kind of notices are inserted to lead to farther discoveries, and if a nobler compendium shall be formed, I willingly resign such minutiae to oblivion." An apology in similar terms is required by this chapter. Indeed, Walpole's very words might meet the case, but that to say that " all kind of notices " are to be found in what follows would be to claim too much.

Responsibility for a great deal of what we admire in the average Stuart or Georgian church rests not with the architect who designed the fabric, but with the craftsmen employed to furnish and ornament it. And as often as not, it must be realized, responsibility in the fullest possible sense ; the exact relationship between architect and craftsman is always hard to determine, but it is probably safe to say that not until the second half of the eighteenth century did it become common for the same man to design both the building and its fittings and furniture. Yet how seldom do we find any record of these craftsmen's names ! Or if the names have, by some chance, come down to us, how seldom do we know anything further about them ! The irony of it is that this posthumous anonymity is due in large measure to the very excellence of their work. Their contemporaries were able to take fine craftsmanship for granted.

Of all the crafts that contribute to the internal effect of the churches we have glanced at in the course of this book, none, perhaps, is more important than that of the joiner and woodcarver. Grinling Gibbons is here the name everyone knows—but he quite certainly, whatever local rumour may say to the contrary, never executed a single piece of wood-carving for any church outside London. Nor did he, court artist that he was, do any of the work popularly attributed to him in the London City churches (St. James's, Piccadilly, of course, not being strictly speaking a City church). This was from the hand of other men, lesser men no doubt and yet of ponderable talents, the Creechers and Cleeres and Emmetts and Maines and Newmans. Here we have at least names because vestry minutes and churchwarden's accounts have come down to us. But in the churches of the provinces there is plenty of work well up to their standard—think of Honington (125) and Ingestre (124, 126) alone—with which we can connect no names at all. Even Willen, where with the aid of Hooke's diary we might surmise that the font-cover (132) was carved by the same Bates that carved the font-cover of

128 Jacobean canopied pews

129 The reredos, c.1680

Rycote chapel, Oxfordshire

130 In the Temple church, Bristol

131 St. Nicholas, Bristol, by William Edney

WOODWORK AND IRONWORK DESTROYED BY BOMBS

St. Anne and St. Agnes, Gresham Street, is the exception. And for the most part the historian of our later church woodwork outside London, should he desire to pass beyond mere names, would have to be content with such exiguous scraps of information as that the John Mitchell who in 1697 received £140 for a reredos for St. Peter's, Bristol, was "a carpenter of London", as the accounts describe him.

The case of decorative ironwork is more than a little similar. The figure who corresponds to Grinling Gibbons here is the great French smith, Jean Tijou, creator of the ironwork in St. Paul's and of the screen and gates by the river at Hampton Court; there are fine altar rails attributed to him at Lydiard Tregoze in Wiltshire. The answer to the question whether or not Tijou was in fact the greatest artist in wrought iron to have worked in England depends to some extent on one's estimate of the limitations of that medium; the baroque ironwork of native craftsmen is, generally speaking, less three-dimensional and more purely linear in conception—but possibly none the worse for that. The provision of gates and railings for houses, both in town and country, probably afforded the most constant source of income for the smith. But churches had to have altar rails, and sometimes screens, or sword-rests to hold the sword of the mayor on his state attendances—among provincial towns Worcester (140), Bristol (141) and Norwich have the best collections of these—and for any or all of these, his services might be required. Yet of all the craftsmen who made ironwork for provincial churches during our period, only two, Bakewell and Edney, come near to emerging from the fogs of time and indifference as recognizable artistic personalities.

Little enough is discoverable about even Robert Bakewell, the Derby smith, who is the more celebrated of the pair. His earliest recorded work was a wrought-iron "arbour" at Melbourne, made in 1707-11 for Thomas Coke, and in connection with this the Coke family correspondence records that in 1708 Bakewell had a shop fitting up at Derby. "He is so miserable poor," says the writer of the letter containing this information, "I believe he cannot remove till he has some money." And with that glimpse of penury our knowledge of the man, aside from his work, would appear to end. Most of the latter was undoubtedly secular; gates at Okeover Hall and others at Etwall Hall, both in Derbyshire, are or were fine examples of his art, and so are the gates he made for Sir Thomas Lombe's silk mill at Derby, which are now set up beside the Derby public library. But nowhere is Bakewell seen to such advantage as in All Saints', Derby. For his great screen with its three pairs of gates, (139) which constitutes the sole baroque flourish in that beautiful, but cold interior, he received £338 10s. It was badly mutilated during some particularly senseless alterations in 1873-4, but has since been restored. The gates made by him for the west end of the churchyard—he received £108 19s. 8d. for them—were less fortunate. They were sold by auction.

Ironwork in a number of other churches may have been wrought by Bakewell. The chancel screen and gates at Staunton Harold (138) are perhaps the most elaborate of the works which are putatively his. The altar rails at Foremark and Weston-under-Lizard have also been attributed to him, and since it is known that he supplied the ironwork for

Worcester Town Hall, of which Thomas White was the architect, it seems not unlikely that he was responsible for the mayoral sword-rests at St. Swithin's and All Saints' (140) in that city, and for the altar rails at Castle Bromwich.

About William Edney information is scarce indeed. One authority states that he "probably worked on the choir screens at St. Paul's", but his name does not appear in the whole length and breadth of the Wren Society's volumes.[1] What is certain, is that he made the superb ironwork in St. Mary Redcliffe, Bristol. This, which dates from 1710, now stands

Castle Bromwich : centre panel of the communion rail

at the west end of the church, but actually comprises a pair of chancel gates and two pairs of gates designed for the sides of the chancel. For the former Edney was paid £60 ; for the latter £50. He also made the screens, gates and sword-rests in two other Bristol churches, the Temple and St. Nicholas' (131). These were equally splendid but have, alas, perished by bomb, so that to find other ironwork by Edney that might be classified as ecclesiastical one must probably go as far afield as Tewkesbury Abbey, where the churchyard gates, erected by Lord Gage in 1734, are attributed to him on stylistic grounds.

* * *

For the sculptor in stone and marble the churches of our period did not offer much scope. Keystone masks, or urns upon the parapet of the tower, or an achievement of arms in a pediment—that is about as much stone ornament, as distinct from standard mouldings and architectural features, as we generally find on the outside of a Stuart or Georgian church. Within, there is the font, of course ; and All Saints', Oxford, boasts the rarity of an elaborate carved ceiling of stone. Above all, there are the monuments. Yet the temptation to write at length of these

[1] A Robert Edney witnessed Grinling Gibbon's signature on an agreement for a monument in 1693.

and of their sculptors is to be resisted here. For although many of the churches mentioned in earlier chapters contain tombs of the greatest interest—Sir Josiah Child's at Wanstead, by John Nost, Lord Foley's at Great Witley, by Michael Rysbrack, Sir Edward Ward's at Stoke Doyle, the veritable museum of monumental sculpture at Croome, and, on a smaller scale, the relief, signed by Grinling Gibbons, to young Robert Cotton at Conington come to mind—these were not conceived as part of the buildings in which they were set up; indeed, many of them antedate their settings by many years.

A minor branch of sculpture which is to be studied in churches, if not so well as elsewhere, is stucco work. *Stucco duro*, introduced into England at Nonesuch Palace in Henry VIII's reign, allowed of the boldest modelling and undercutting. English taste, however, for a long time favoured rather low relief, as may be seen in work as late as the roof panels of St. John's, Leeds (6). For stucco work of the second half of seventeenth century, by which time a fully-fledged baroque style mingling naturalistic detail with Louis Quatorze *motifs* was established, the churches of Ingestre (146), Euston (143), and All Saints', Northampton (19) may be cited; the craftsmen are not known.

But the most splendid ecclesiastical ceiling outside London surviving from this period is that of the church of St. Charles the Martyr, Tunbridge Wells (143), which bears the dates 1682 and 1690. It was executed, and maybe designed, by Henry Doogood and John Wetherill, who received £190 for their pains.

Doogood was one of Wren's two principal plasterers, employed by him at St. Paul's, at many of the City churches, and (with John Grove) at Trinity College Library, Cambridge. Wetherill also worked for Wren—at Greenwich Hospital, for instance. Their ceiling at Tunbridge Wells, with its miniature domes and compartments (145), is distinctly old-fashioned for its date; quite un-Frenchified, it harks back to the days of Inigo Jones and Webb.

Of Georgian stucco there is a fair amount in churches up and down the land. During the first third or so of the eighteenth century, provincial work still exhibited the fruit and flowers of the baroque, as in the ceiling of the chancel at Gayhurst (38). But already in the 'twenties the rococo had arrived, with the persons of Artari and Bagutti, who were brought from Italy by Gibbs to decorate St. Martin's-in-the-Fields and Marylebone Chapel. They are a mysterious pair, belonging to that too large class of the famous obscure. Much domestic work is connected with their names, either together or singly; Houghton, Mawley Hall (in Shropshire), Sutton Scarsdale and Mereworth are among the houses concerned. The stucco work in Great Witley church (144, 150) is attributed to Bagutti mainly because he is known, on the authority of Defoe (who called him Pargotti), to have executed that in the chapel at Canons, whence came the paintings by Bellucci for which it forms the setting. About the middle of the century a native rococo appeared, and flourished particularly in the south-west and in the north. Thomas Stocking of Bristol, who was responsible for the ceiling of St. Nicholas' in that city, must have been among the chief practitioners of the former school. But little enough is known about him. He carried out work to the value of £570 at Corsham Court and other work, it would appear, at Arno's Castle, Brislington, and he died, "esteemed and respected", in 1806.

* * *

If the sculptor's opportunities in an Anglican church were limited, the painter's were even more so. In early Stuart times they were confined to heraldry and the painting of the Ten Commandments and other texts: H. Munro Cautley, in *Royal Arms and Commandments in our Churches*, quotes a licence issued by Archbishop Abbot in 1631 to the painter-stainer Thomas Hanbage, authorizing him to visit churches to carry out this kind of work and "wishing . . . all Persons, Vicars, Curats, Church-wardens, Sidesmen, and all other officers of the severall churches aforesaid that they to their best powers give you admittance as is fit in the performance of the premisses". After the Restoration a modest English school of baroque decorators found some employment in Wren's churches. This school culminated in the work of Sir James Thornhill, but neither he nor the lesser but still interesting artist Robert Streater, painter of the ceiling of the Sheldonian at Oxford, is represented in any provincial church. There are, however, a few painted church ceilings of the later seventeenth century by local artists, such as that over the nave at Staunton Harold, (said to be the work of one Melbourne)—a sombre and menacing sky with turgid clouds parting to reveal the sacred name at the eastern end—or the very delightful one (dating from 1671) over the chancel at Bromfield, Shropshire (147), where the heavens are a-flutter with angels and text-bearing streamers.

One of the earliest arrivals among those foreigners whose invasion so much enriched the arts in England during the baroque period, was the painter Louis Laguerre, who has a place in this book by virtue of his decorations at Little Stanmore or Whitchurch (25, 148, 149). Laguerre was born in Paris, son of a Catalan who was Louis XIV's *maître de la menagerie*, and after education at the Jesuits' College became a pupil of Charles le Brun. He came to England in 1683, at the age of twenty, and stayed for the remaining thirty-eight years of his life, dying of an apoplectic fit in Drury Lane theatre, whither he had gone to see a benefit performance for his son John, who, in Walpole's words, "had talents for painting, but wanted application, preferring the stage to more laborious studies". Louis Laguerre's first wife—he was twice married—was Jean Tijou's daughter.

Laguerre was for many years chief assistant to Antonio Verrio, with whom, thanks to Pope, in most minds he is inseparably bracketed. He had, however, an artistic personality of his own, and may be reckoned the better painter of the pair. His masterpiece is probably to be found in the saloon at Blenheim, which has architecturally treated walls and a ceiling "emblematically representing John, Duke of Marlborough in the career of victory, arrested by the hand of Peace", as the eighteenth-century guide-book puts it. Laguerre was to have painted the dome of St. Paul's, but as everyone knows the commission eventually went to Thornhill. The subjects of his paintings in the nave at Little Stanmore

132 Willen, Buckinghamshire, c.1679

133 Castle Bromwich, Warwickshire, c.1731

134 Croome d'Abitot, Worcestershire, c.1763

135 Teigh, Rutland, c.1782

FOUR FONTS

136 Two tier candelabrum, Knutsford, Cheshire, c.1745

137 The communion table, Wheatfield, Oxfordshire, c.1740

have been enumerated in Chapter II. Yet it is arguable that his best work there is not in the body of the church but in the mausoleum abutting it on the north. Here are no scriptural subjects, but walls and ceiling are painted with an architectural scheme comprising sham columns, statues in niches, urns, *putti*, and a dome (149). The whole *ensemble* constitutes a skilful piece of baroque deception, which can still take the unprepared spectator by surprise.

As we have seen, it is to the patronage of the same Duke of Chandos who rebuilt Little Stanmore church that we owe the only other full-scale baroque decorations to be found in a church outside London—the paintings executed by Bellucci for the private chapel at Canons about 1720 and transferred by Lord Foley to Great Witley in or after 1747 (150). Antonio Bellucci was born at Soligo, near Venice, in 1654. He worked at Venice and Verona, at Vienna for Charles VI, and at the court of the Elector Palatine; it was not till 1716 that he came to England. His biggest commission here was the decoration of the staircase of Buckingham House, for which he received £500. This was completed in 1722 and in the same year he left the country, " being afflicted with the gout", to die in his native town four years later.

Bellucci's paintings at Witley are the work of a decorator of very great talent. They are less dry in manner than Laguerre's at Stanmore (148, 149), and better composed and more harmonious in colour than anything by Verrio at Hampton Court. Altogether there are twenty-three of them, but twenty are merely small panels of angels and cherubs (144). The subjects of the larger paintings (from east to west) are the Nativity, the Ascension (150), and the Deposition.

The other painter responsible, if in less direct fashion, for the baroque splendours of Great Witley was Sebastiano Ricci, who designed the windows executed by Joshua Price. Ricci was a skilful *pasticheur* who was especially esteemed for his imitations of Paolo Veronese, which he is said to have passed off on occasion as works of that master himself. Though here of course the mediation of Price and the technique of painted glass diminish the resemblance, several of the Witley windows are in the manner of Veronese; that depicting the Adoration of the Magi, for instance, might be a simplified and emasculated version of Veronese's painting of the same subject now in the National Gallery. And with that picture, indeed, Ricci would probably have been familiar, for it was then in the church of San Silvestro, Venice, and Ricci was a native of Belluno. Bellucci's junior by some six years, he worked in Italy and in Vienna, where he carried out decorative schemes at the imperial palace of Schoenbrunn, and came to England at the suggestion of his nephew, Marco Ricci. During the decade he spent in the country he decorated the chapel at Bulstrode (long destroyed), and painted the ceiling roundels in the hall at Burlington House and the altar-piece at Chelsea Hospital; he also worked for Queen Anne at Hampton Court. The story goes that he left in a pique because he was not commissioned to decorate the dome of St. Paul's.

The last baroque decorator with whom we are concerned was also an Italian—this time a Milanese. Josephi Borgnis, who painted the Last

Supper on the ceiling of the chancel at West Wycombe, first became acquainted with Sir Francis Dashwood when the latter was in Italy on the Grand Tour in 1726. Ten years later Dashwood visited Italy again; this time when he returned to England the painter came with him, to settle at West Wycombe under his patronage. Borgnis' most extensive works may still be studied in the murals and ceilings at West Wycombe Park; his most curious, the decorations of the chapel at Medmenham Abbey, where Dashwood and his cronies foregathered to celebrate Black Mass, have long been destroyed. His painting in West Wycombe church, a somewhat enigmatic version of its subject in which Judas Iscariot becomes the principal figure, dates from 1761. In the same year he died, and Dashwood put up a tablet to his memory, "*Pictoris Insignis moribus candidis Ornati*", in the mausoleum east of the church.

* * *

A number of eighteenth-century churches contain pictures by other painters besides these, while the passing of the church building act of 1818 was followed by something of a campaign, with James Elmes and Benjamin Robert Haydon as its pamphleteers, to press the art into the service of religion—or religion into the service of the art; it was proposed that a certain percentage of the funds for each new church should be set aside for the commissioning of an altar-piece. But such pictures as found their way into churches during this later period, being easel-paintings, are incidental features which hardly concern us here.

However, there is another kind of pictorial art which does demand consideration. To all but a handful of specialists it is practically an unknown art; the fact may be some excuse for giving fairly full accounts of its practitioners, even if some of the information seems not altogether relevant to our main subject. Anything which can arouse interest in them is, one may feel, of value, for no art has of late years been so little regarded as theirs. Indeed, a caveat must here be entered, to the effect that the mention of any individual works in the following pages is not to be taken as implying that they still exist; in many cases a personal check has not been possible and there is generally no other way of telling whether they do or not. With this necessary preface, a section,—the last section—of this book may be devoted to the artists and art of Stuart and Georgian stained glass.

It has little in common with medieval stained glass, as its detractors never weary of telling us. (But that is really no reason for despising or neglecting it; the first rule of criticism is to accept works of art for what they are and not to reject them for what they are not.) Part of the difference is technical; medieval stained glass windows were composed of glass coloured in the mass, or *pot-metal*, while later windows were largely, and sometimes entirely, of clear glass painted with vitrifiable enamels. It is usual to explain this change as due to Louis XIII's destruction of the glass furnaces of Lorraine in 1634. But in reality the use of enamels was by then already well established, and, although that historical accident deprived Europe of the main source of its supply of coloured glass, the only medieval process whose secret appears to have

Copyright " Country Life Ltd."

138 The chancel screen and gates, c.1720, Staunton Harold, Leicestershire, probably by Robert Bakewell

139 Centre gates of screen, All Saints, Derby (now the cathedral), c.1725, by Robert Bakewell

140 Sword rest, All Saints, Worcester, c.1736

141 Sword rest, St. Paul's, Bristol

142 Communion rail, coloured and gilt, c.1710, Weston, Staffordshire

been generally lost for a time was the manufacture of "flashed ruby";[1] pot-metal was always manufactured here and there, the chief English centre in the eighteenth century being Stourbridge. The simple fact is that the seventeenth and eighteenth centuries liked enamels because they wanted their windows to resemble oil paintings—in the same way as the early Middle Ages, one may suppose, wanted theirs to resemble manuscript illuminations—and enamels made this possible.

An Ordinance of Queen Elizabeth had required the destruction of "superstitious" glass paintings and the substitution of plain glass. Nevertheless, heraldic windows continued to be set up and early in the seventeenth century windows depicting religious subjects crept back. But with a few exceptions, such as the east window at Abbey Dore, the most remarkable examples of the latter are to be found not in parish churches but in High Church and still half medieval Oxford. Here the most celebrated artists were two Flemings, Bernard and Abraham Van Linge; Bernard's work may be studied best in the chapel at Wadham and Abraham's at University College.

The Commonwealth must have been a serious set-back for the glass-painters. But after the Restoration their art came into its own again—or, if that is saying too much, at any rate was in moderate demand. The first English glass-painter of whose character and mode of life it is possible to reconstruct a coherent picture is Henry Gyles (1645-1709) of York.

The documents in the case are the letters of the antiquary Ralph Thoresby and some of Gyles's own letters that have survived and are now in the British Museum. Son of Edmund Gyles, who was also a glass-painter, and numbering other glass-painters among his forebears, Henry Gyles would have been described by Dr. Johnson as a clubbable man, and his house in Micklegate, York, was the rendezvous of a circle which included, besides Thoresby, the etcher and pioneer mezzotint engraver Francis Place, the architect Etty, the zoologist Martin Lister, and the heraldic painter and genealogist Sylvanus Morgan. Everyone appears to have liked Gyles; and towards the end of his life, when he was very poor and racked by gout into the bargain, his friends were in the habit of making him presents of money. He had himself always been generous, while the price of his work seems to have been reckoned more often in shillings than in pounds. There can be little doubt but that most of this work was of a secular nature, ranging from small panels for gentlemen's cabinets to the royal arms in the north window of Trinity library at Cambridge, of which Gyles wrote to Thoresby that he had heard that it was "highly approved of and looked on as a very curious ornament to the College and far beyond anything they have seen done in glass-painting". ("But, alack! Sir," he added "what avails it to have a man's labours praised if the reward for them will not keep him from want," and in another letter he exclaims, in somewhat Puginesque phrase, "Masters of Art? No greater enemies to Art!") Of windows by him depicting specifically religious subjects, only two are recorded—a Nativity in the chapel of

[1] Red glass of the thickness necessary for windows is practically opaque. Therefore a thin layer of it (say 1/16 of an inch) would be applied, or "flashed on" to sheets of clear glass.

University College, Oxford, painted about 1682, and a King David and St. Cecilia in the church at Denton, Yorkshire (151), dated 1700. For the former, which was removed by Sir Gilbert Scott, Gyles apparently made his own glass. Knowledge of technical processes had been handed down through his family, and a letter to him from Dr. John Place, physician to the Grand Duke of Tuscany and cousin of the engraver, whom he had asked to enquire for coloured glass in Italy, shows that he knew the secret of flashed ruby. Other churches besides Denton known to contain glass by Gyles are Adel (armorial window of 1681 and inscribed window of 1706) and Stillingfleet (armorial, 1698).

Although Thoresby called him "the famousest painter of glass perhaps in the world", the truth is that Gyles, who "worked mostly in monochrome touched up with yellow stain and a few lifeless enamels, his best colour being a somewhat dull blue",[1] was a not very considerable artist, although his windows are of some historical interest.

William Price the elder (d.1722) and his brother Joshua Price are said to have been pupils of Henry Gyles. With William we are not really concerned, since it appears that no works by him in parish churches are known, although in company with most of the notable glass-painters of our period he was employed at Oxford, where he painted the main lights of the east window of Merton College chapel. And Joshua is anyhow the more important artist. For Oxford he painted, in 1715, a Holy Family in the east window of the chapel at Queen's College. Three years later he painted the east window of St. Andrew's, Holborn, showing the Last Supper in the three lower lights and the Resurrection above; this was destroyed in the blitz. Between doing the Queen's and Holborn windows he restored and added to the windows of Denton church, near Bungay, but the most important remaining work by Joshua Price is the series of ten windows to Sebastiano Ricci's design executed for the chapel at Canons and now at Great Witley. The subjects of these are (east window) Resurrection; (north transept) the healing of the lame man by Saints Peter and John; (north side of nave) Baptism in Jordan, Adoration of the Magi, Arrival at the Inn; (south side of nave) St. Peter walking on the waters, Adoration of the Shepherds, Annunciation; (west gallery) the Israelites sacrificing to the golden calf, the marriage at Cana (153).

The larger windows, except St. Peter on the waters and the Annunciation, are signed J. Price 1721. In translating Ricci's designs into terms of glass Price used both enamels and pot-metal. The former technique predominates in all the windows, but most of the draperies are cut out of sheets of glass coloured in the mass and leaded round. The effect is very rich and the quality of the glass lends weight to the claims made by the Price brothers in an advertisement:

"Whereas the ancient Art of Painting and Staining Glass has been much discouraged, by reason of an opinion generally received that the *Red Colour* (not made in Europe for many years) is totally lost; these are to give notice, that the said *Red* and all other colours are made to as great a degree of Curiosity and Fineness as in former Ages by William

[1] J. A. Knowles, Walpole Society, Vol. XI.

143 Euston, Suffolk: ceiling to south aisle, 1676

144 Great Witley, Worcestershire: detail of ceiling cove, 1747 or after

145 Detail of Plaster ceiling 1682-90, St. Charles the Martyr, Tunbridge Wells, by Henry Doogood and John Wetherill

146 The chancel ceiling, c.1676, Ingestre, Staffordshire

147 Bromfield, Shropshire: the chancel ceiling, 1671

148 Saints and prophets, in grisaille, in the nave

149 The mausoleum ceiling.

Paintings by Louis Laguerre at Little Stanmore, Middlesex, c.1714

and Joshua Price Glaziers and Glass-Painters, near Hatton Garden in Holborn, London; where Gentlemen may have Church History, etc., Painted upon Glass in what colours they please, to as great Perfection as ever . . ."

Joshua Price had a son William who practised the same art. But the best glass-painter of the succeeding generation was William Peckitt (1731-1795). He was another native of York and his father was a glove-maker; what led him to take up glass-painting and where he learnt the rudiments of the art are matters for conjecture. He is first met with in 1752, when he advertises in the *York Courant* to inform "all gentlemen, clergymen and others that by many experiments he has found out the art of painting or staining of glass in all kinds of colours and all sorts of Figures". In the same year he presented to the York Corporation a window depicting Justice in a Triumphal Car and the city arms, in return for which he was made a freeman without payment. In 1763 he married Mary Mitley, daughter of a prominent local sculptor. Towards the end of his life he became devout, and wrote a number of treatises on religious subjects, one of which has survived in printed form.

Peckitt's ecclesiastical work included windows at Coxwold (Fauconberg arms, 1755), York minster (west window on south side of nave, Saints Peter and John, 1758, and window in south transept (152), Lincoln Cathedral (east window, 1762, and another, both removed), New College chapel, Oxford (four windows), Glynde church (east window, 1765), Exeter Cathedral (west window, 1766, removed 1904), St. John's, Manchester (east window, Saints John, Peter and James, 1769, presumably destroyed with the church), Rothwell (east window, 1770), Binley (east window, Holy Family, 1776), St. James's, Sheffield (east window, 1788), and Yarm (Moses delivering the Law). According to Winston, Peckitt's east window at Lincoln contained the last flashed ruby glass used in England before its rediscovery in 1826. His work is always worth looking for—and at; he is a minor artist who deserves a monograph.

Like the Prices, Peckitt used a certain amount of pot-metal in his windows. Francis Eginton, who for two decades at the end of the eighteenth century and the opening of the nineteenth was without question the most celebrated and the most prolific of English glass-painters, worked almost exclusively in enamels.

Eginton set up as a glass-painter at Handsworth, near Birmingham, in 1784. Of unknown origin, he enters history as superintendent of the japanned ware department in Matthew Boulton's Soho factory, where he was employed also in modelling and in taking casts of statuettes and other objects which Boulton borrowed for reproduction. Then in 1777 he comes to the fore as the inventor of "polygraphs" or "sun-pictures," as they were called, by which oil paintings up to a fair size were reproduced in colour with considerable fidelity. The discovery in 1863 of two photographic plates among some old papers of the Boulton firm started a silly theory that these "sun-pictures" were photographs. The truth is that they were aquatints, printed in colour and worked up by hand.

The polygraphs played an important part in Eginton's life, for their failure to pay their way led to the dissolution of his partnership with

Boulton. Before that, there had been a move to get him a pension from the government, but Boulton put a stop to the scheme with a letter to Lord Dartmouth, in which he wrote: " . . . it might perhaps be injurious to me, as such a pension would tend to make him more independent of me and my manufacture. His attachment to me, his knowing that no use hath been made of the things, the obligation he is under to me, and his own natural caution and prudence, renders me firmly persuaded that the scheme will die away in his memory, or at least will never be mentioned. If anybody is entitled to any pecuniary reward in this business, it is myself . . . " It is evident that Eginton never knew what had passed. He remained on the best of terms with his old employer, who supplied him with plates from which to continue the production of polygraphs at Prospect Hill House, Handsworth—where, in addition to painting glass, he conducted a trade in japanned tin, iron wares, and buttons.

Eginton's studio was one of the show-places of Birmingham. In 1802 it was inspected by Lord Nelson, accompanied by Sir William and Lady Hamilton; the path of the distinguished visitors was strewn with flowers by a number of the prettiest girls of the district. Eginton's glass painting must have been a profitable business; the list of works for which he is known to have been responsible is impressive. It is interesting to note that in the first window he ever painted, it is said, he transferred an impression from one of his polygraph plates to the glass and then finished it with enamels. He was hardly an original artist. Nearly all his subject windows appear to have been copied from paintings by recognized masters, ancient or modern. Thus his biggest commission consisted of fifty subjects after Gavin Hamilton at Fonthill, and his largest single window, a Resurrection in Salisbury Cathedral, was after Reynolds. The east window of St. Paul's, Birmingham, set up in 1791 and perhaps his most important work surviving in a parish church, was copied from a painting by Benjamin West, which Eginton hired for eighty guineas. The President of the Royal Academy, in a letter accompanying his picture, wrote in mock-scriptural style: " Then may these Works which Francis Eginton hath made manifest to the World, chear the sight of those unborn that Generations yet to come may know the goodly things that were done, in the days of our good King Azakiah." But it must be many years since anyone's sight was cheered, precisely, by Eginton's window. At the best of times it was considered desirable to draw curtains over the side windows of the chancel to see it to advantage, and now the grime of Birmingham has rendered its never too translucent enamels all but completely opaque.

Eginton's east window at St. Alkmund's, Shrewsbury, is more visible. Showing a figure of Faith, after a painting by Guido Reni, and dated 1795, it is rather garish in colour and pitched in a high key. Nevertheless, it was " executed in a manner highly satisfactory to the Trustees " and the artist received £200 for it. Of about the same date was the east window at Wanstead. Its subject was Christ bearing the Cross, after Ribalti's altar-piece at Magdalen College, Oxford; it is now to be seen only in the portrait of Eginton, painted by James Millar in 1796, in the Birmingham Art Gallery. Among other churches which contain, or did once contain,

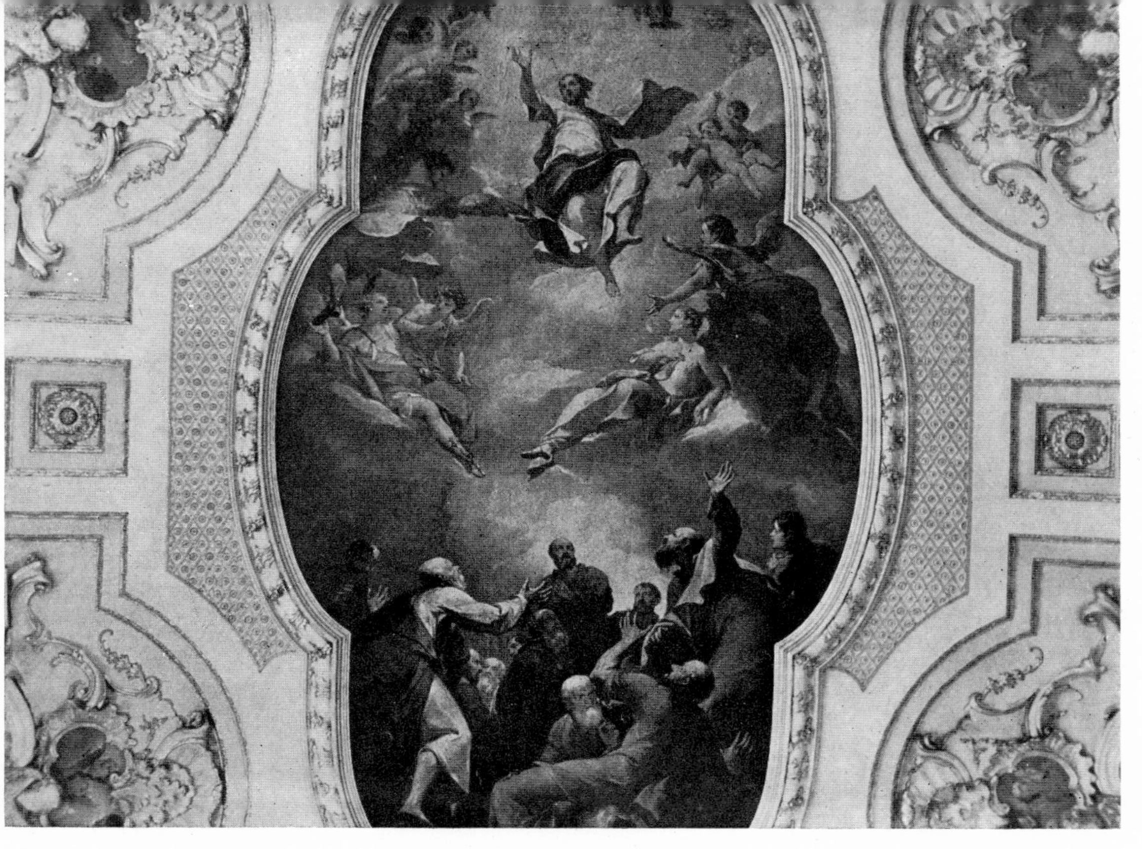

150 Great Witley, Worcestershire : ceiling painting over centre of nave, by Antonio Bellucci, executed c.1719 for the private chapel at Canons, Middlesex *The Ascension*

151 Fairfax chapel window, Denton-on-Wharfedale, Yorkshire, 1702, by Henry Gyles, *King David and St. Cecilia*

152 Glass by William Peckitt in the south transept, York Minster *King Solomon*

153 Detail of window at Great Witley, Worcestershire: glass dated 1721, by Joshua Price after a design by Sebastiano Ricci, originally at Canons, Middlesex *The*

works by Eginton are Aston, near Birmingham ; Babworth, Nottinghamshire ; Barr and Bromley Regis, Staffordshire ; Buckingham ; Frome, Somerset ; Hatton, Warwickshire ; Papplewick, near Nottingham ; Shrivenham, Somerset ; Shugborough, Staffordshire, and Tewkesbury Abbey.

Eginton had two pupils, Thomas Philip and Henry Wyatt (both of whom became portrait-painters) and an assistant, Samuel Lowe, who became his son-in-law and who after his death carried on his style of glass painting in enamels. The baroque tradition of stained glass had other nineteenth-century followers, such as Collins, who executed the Ascension in the east window of William Burgess's church of St. Sidwell, Exeter (1813)—" without that due attention to propriety required in a christian temple ", an early cicerone primly comments—and David Evans of Shrewsbury, whose richly coloured glass in the Venetian east window of St. Chad's in his native town, after a Deposition by Rubens, dates from as late as 1838. By the 1820's, though, the most significant development was not along these lines, but in the direction of a revived medievalism.

Thomas Willement was the leader of the new school. Born in 1786, he was by type a gentleman-antiquary, and his first appointment was as heraldic artist to George IV ; in 1832 he was elected F.S.A. He began to paint glass, it would appear, in 1812, for that is the date of the earliest work named in *A concise Account of the Principal Works in Stained Glass . . . by Thomas Willement*, which, published in 1840, makes him one of the best documented of artists in the medium. Between the first mentioned date and 1837 he had supplied windows for nearly three dozen churches besides other buildings, while in the opening years of Queen Victoria's reign he was if anything kept even busier. Provincial churches listed in the *Concise Account* include St. George's, Tyldesley ; Maidenhead ; Seale ; Begbrook ; Bilston ; Orsett ; Wroxham ; Holy Trinity, Brighton ; Snodland ; Tabley ; Layer Marney ; Butleigh ; Arundel ; Cockayne Hatley ; Chenies ; Mamhead ; Haytor ; Ripon Minster ; Northchurch ; Adderbury; Ashford; Tyneham; Tortington; Great Bedwyn; Cresswell; North Cray ; Hampton Lucy . . . . but anyone who may have a curiosity to follow up this neglected subject is referred to the volume itself. The unprejudiced eye will find charm and even beauty in some at any rate of Willement's work. Historically, his importance resides in the fact that he was the first to bring real medieval scholarship to the design of stained glass. When he died, in 1871, the Athenæum said that " modern glass-painters are to a considerable extent indebted [to him] for the revival of their art in that manner which, if not the best, was probably the only practicable one." Perhaps one might call Willement the father of Victorian glass-painting. If so, his is a heavy responsibility.

LIST OF STUART AND GEORGIAN CHURCHES ARRANGED UNDER COUNTIES

The following list includes all Stuart and Georgian churches mentioned or illustrated in this book. It pretends to no other kind of completeness whatsoever. I have visited many churches not included in it, but I shall be glad to hear of any really outstanding examples which I may have missed. No general list of churches of the period is available. *Kelly's Directory* is often the best guide to any given area, since it is free from the prejudices endemic among more " literary " guide-books.

Double dates denote the period of construction, as elsewhere in this book. For the precise significance of single dates the reader is referred to the main text. The names of the architects are given when known to me. A number of attributions are also given, but attributions suggested for the first time in this book are not.

Abbreviations.

(G.) : (revived) Gothic. (d.) : destroyed or demolished. (att.) : attributed to.

Berkshire

Hungerford, 1814-16, J. Pinch, (G.)
Theale, 1820-32, E. Garbett, (G.)

Buckinghamshire

Biddlesden, c. 1730
Buckingham, 1780, (G.), (remodelled)
Fulmer, 1610
Gayhurst, 1728
Hartwell, 1753-56, H. Keene, (G.)
Old Wolverton, 1815, T. Hakewill, (G.)
Stony Stratford, 1776, F. Hiorn, (G.)
Tyringham, c. 1796, J. Soane, (design not executed)
West Wycombe, 1763

Cambridgeshire

Conington, 1737
Cottenham, tower 1617
Wimpole, 1749, H. Flitcroft, (much altered)

Cheshire

Congleton, St. Peter, 1742
Eccleston, 1809, W. Porden, (G.), (d.)
Knutsford, St. John the Baptist, 1744
Lower Whitley, 1620
Stockport, St. Thomas, 1825, G. Basevi

Cornwall

Helston, 1756-61, Bland ; tower, Edwards
Penzance, St. Mary, 1834, C. Hutchins, (G.)

DERBYSHIRE

Derby, All Saints (now the Cathedral), 1723-25, J. Gibbs

DEVON

Exeter, St. David, 1816, J. Green, (d.)
Plymouth, St. Andrew, 1823, J. Foulston
Teigngrace, 1787, (G.)
Werrington, 1740, (G.)

DORSET

Blandford, 1731-39, J. Bastard
Charlton Marshall, 1715, Bastard
Portland, St. George Reforne, 1777, Gilbert

DURHAM COUNTY

Sedgefield, fittings 1635

ESSEX

Colchester, St. Mary at the Walls, 1714, J. Price, (d.)
Mistley, 1766, R. Adam (all but towers d.)
Wanstead, 1790, T. Hardwick

GLOUCESTERSHIRE

Badminton, 1786
Bristol:
  Christ Church, 1792, W. Paty
  Redlands Green, 1743, J. Strachan
  St. George, Brandon Hill, 1823, R. Smirke
  St. Michael, 1775-77, T. Paty, (G.)
  St. Nicholas, 1762-68, J. Bridges, (G.), (d.)
  St. Paul, 1789-95, D. Hague, (G).
  St. Thomas, 1793, J. Allen
Clifton, Holy Trinity, 1829, C. R. Cockerell
Dodington, 1803, J. Wyatt
Flaxley, c. 1780, A. Keck, (d.)
Newent, nave 1675-79, E. Taylor
Tetbury, 1777-81, F. Hiorn, (G.)

HAMPSHIRE

Avington, 1779
Hale, c. 1720, att. T. Archer
Portsmouth, St. Paul, 1820-22, F. Goodwin
Southampton, All Saints', 1790, W. Reveley, (d.)
Strathfieldsaye, 1784

HEREFORDSHIRE

Abbey Dore, fittings 1634, att. J. Abel
Monnington-on-Wye, 1679-80
Shobdon, 1753, (G.)
Stoke Edith, 1740
Tyberton, 1720

HERTFORDSHIRE
Ayot St. Lawrence, 1778-79, N. Revett
Buntingford, St. Peter, 1615

HUNTINGDONSHIRE
Leighton Bromswold, 1626-34
Little Gidding, chancel possibly 1625, rest of church mainly 1714

KENT
Groombridge, 1623
Mereworth, 1744-46
Riverhead, c. 1825, D. Burton, (G.)
Shipbourne, 1721, J. Gibbs, (d.)
Southborough, 1830, D. Burton, (G.)
Strood, St. Nicholas, 1814, R. Smirke
Tunbridge Wells:
  Charles the Martyr, 1682-90
  Holy Trinity, 1827, D. Burton, (G.)

LANCASHIRE
Liverpool:
  St. Luke, 1810-31, J. Foster, (G.), (d.)
  St. Michael, Pitt Street, 1816-26, J. Foster, (d.)
  St. Nicholas, body of church, 1774-75, J. Brooker, (d.), tower 1811, J. Harrison
  St. Paul, 1769, T. Lightholler, (d.)
Manchester:
  St. George, Hulme, 1826, F. Goodwin, (G.)
  St. John, 1769, (G.), (d.)
  St. Matthew, Campfield, 1822-25, C. Barry, (G.)
  St. Peter, 1788-94, J. Wyatt, (d.)
Preston, St. Peter, 1823-25, T. Rickman, (G.)
Salford, St. Philip, 1825, R. Smirke

LEICESTERSHIRE
Galby, 1741, Wing senior, (G.)
King's Norton, 1770, Wing junior, (G.)
Saxby, 1788
Stapleford, 1783, G. Richardson, (G.)
Staunton Harold, 1653-63

LINCOLNSHIRE
Gainsborough, All Saints', 1736-48
Stamford, St. Michael, 1836, J. Brown, (G.)

MIDDLESEX
Hanworth, 1812, J. Wyatt, (completely altered)
Stanmore, Little (or Whitchurch), 1714-15, J. Price
Stanmore, Great, 1632, (in ruins)
Twickenham, 1714, J. James

NORFOLK
Gunton, 1769, R. Adam
North Runcton, 1713, H. Bell
Yarmouth, St. George, 1714, J. Price

NORTHAMPTONSHIRE
Aynho, 1723
Daventry, 1752, W. and D. Hiorn
Great Houghton, 1754
Northampton, All Saints, 1676-80, att. H. Jones
Steane, 1620
Stoke Doyle, 1722
Wicken, 1758, T. Prowse, (G.)

NORTHUMBERLAND
Newcastle-on-Tyne, All Saints, 1786-96, D. Stephenson

NOTTINGHAMSHIRE
Markham Clinton, 1833, R. Smirke
Nottingham, St. Paul, W. Wilkins, 1822, (d.)
Papplewick, 1785, (G.)

OXFORDSHIRE
Banbury, 1790-97, S. P. Cockerell ; tower 1822, C. R. Cockerell
Chiselhampton, 1763
Churchill, 1826, T. Plowman, (G.)
Nuneham Courtenay, 1764, J. Stuart
Oxford, All Saints, 1707-10, H. Aldrich
Rycote Chapel, fittings, 1620-80
Wheatfield, 1740

RUTLAND
Normanton Park, tower 1826, T. Cundy, (earlier nave rebuilt)
Teigh, 1782, (G.)

SHROPSHIRE
Bridgnorth, 1798, T. Telford
Minsterley, 1692
Shrewsbury :
St. Chad, 1790-92, G. Steuart
St. Alkmund, 1795, Carline and Tilley, (G.)
St. Julian, 1749, T. F. Pritchard
Wellington, 1788, G. Steuart
Whitchurch, 1712-13, W. Smith

SOMERSET
Babington, 1750, att. J. Strachan
Bathwick, 1814-20, J. Pinch
Berkley, 1751
Woolley, 1761, J. Wood, junior

STAFFORDSHIRE
Bilston, St. Leonard, 1826, F. Goodwin
Burton-on-Trent, 1719-26, F. Smith
Ingestre, 1673-76, att. C. Wren
Patshull, 1742, J. Gibbs
Stone, 1754, W. Baker, (G.)
Walsall, St. Matthew, 1820, F. Goodwin, (G.)
West Bromwich, 1821-27, F. Goodwin, (G.)
Weston-under-Lizard, 1700, att. W. Wilson
Wolverhampton, St. John, 1755-60, W. Baker

SUFFOLK

Euston, 1676

SURREY

Guildford, Holy Trinity, 1749
Long Ditton, 1776, R. Taylor, (d.)

SUSSEX

Brighton, St. Peter, 1823-28, C. Barry, (G.)
Chichester, St. John, 1812, J. Elmes
Glynde, 1765, T. Robinson
Hove, St. Andrew, 1824-26, C. Barry
Worthing, St. Paul, 1812, Rebecca

WARWICKSHIRE

Alcester, 1729-33, E. and T. Woodward
Binley, 1771-73, att. R. Adam
Birmingham :
St. Bartholomew, 1749, W. and D. Hiorn, (d.)
St. George, 1819-21, T. Rickman, (G.)
Holy Trinity, Bordesley, 1823, F. Goodwin
St. Mary, 1772-75, (d.)
St. Paul, 1777-79, R. Eykyn
St. Philip (now the Cathedral), 1709-15, T. Archer
St. Peter, Dale End, 1825-27, T. Rickman
St. Thomas, Edgbaston, 1826-29, T. Rickman
Castle Bromwich, 1726-31, att. T. White
Compton Wyngates, 1663
Coventry, Christchurch, 1829-32, T. Rickman
Great Packington, 1790, J. Bonomi
Hampton, Lucy, 1822-26, T. Rickman
Honily, 1723
Honington, c. 1690
Kineton, c. 1750, S. Miller, (G.), remodelled
Over Whitacre, 1766
Preston-on-Stour, 1752-57, (G.)
Warwick :
St. Mary, nave and tower 1694-1704, W. Wilson
St. Nicholas, tower 1748, T. Johnson, nave 1779-80, (G.)

WILTSHIRE

Farley, c. 1690, att. C. Wren
Fonthill Gifford, c. 1760, (d.)
Hardenhuish, 1779, J. Wood, junior

WORCESTERSHIRE

Croome D'Abitot, 1763, (G.)
Dudley :
St. Edmund, 1724
St. Thomas, 1817, W. Brooks, (G.)
Great Witley, 1735
Hartlebury, 1836-37, T. Rickman, (G.)
Ombersley, 1825-29, T. Rickman, (G.)

WORCESTERSHIRE (*continued*)

Rushock, 1758, (G.)
Stanford-on-Teme, 1768, (G.)
Stourbridge, St. Thomas, 1726
Worcester:
  All Saints', 1738-42, T. White
  St. Martin, 1768-72, A. Keck
  St. Nicholas, 1726-30, T. White
  St. Swithin, 1734-36, E. and T. Woodward
Tardebigge, 1777, F. Hiorn

YORKSHIRE

Attercliffe-cum-Darnal, 1822, J. Taylor, (G.)
Bradford, Christ Church, 1815, J. Taylor, (G.), (d.)
Bishopthorpe, 1766, att. T. Atkinson, (G.)
Brandsby-cum-Stearsby, 1767, T. Atkinson
Horbury, 1791, J. Carr
Kirkleatham, 1763, R. Corney
Leeds:
  Christ Church, Meadow Lane, 1823-26, R. D. Chantrell, (G.)
  Holy Trinity, 1721-27, W. Halfpenny
  St. John, 1632-33
  St. Mark, Woodhouse, 1823-26, Atkinson and Sharp, (G.)
  St. Mary, Quarry Hill, 1823-27, J. Taylor (G.)
  St. Paul, 1793, (d.)
Rokeby, 1778, T. Robinson
Scarborough, 1826, Atkinson and Sharp, (G.)
Sheffield:
  St. George, 1821-25, Woodhead and Hurst, (G.)
  St. Paul, 1720-40, G. Platt

INDEX